THE THIRTY MINUTE DINNER

THE THIRTY MINUTE DINNER

by Hannah G. Scheel

Nash Publishing
Los Angeles

BY HANNAH G. SCHEEL:
The One Pot Dinner

Copyright © 1971 by Hannah G. Scheel

All rights reserved. No part of this book
may be reproduced in any form or by any means
without permission in writing from the publisher.

Library of Congress Catalog Card Number: 73-143019
Standard Book Number: 8402-1184-8

Published simultaneously in the United States and
Canada by Nash Publishing, 9255 Sunset Boulevard,
Los Angeles, California 90069.

Printed in the United States of America

First printing

CONTENTS

Foreword *6*
Seafood *13*
Beef *53*
Chicken *119*
Frankfurters *149*
Lamb *165*
Pork *181*
Veal *207*
Variety Meats *225*
Late Suppers *243*

FOREWORD

Only too happily agreeing with Samuel Johnson, who once said, "A man is in general better pleased when he has a good dinner on his table, than when his wife talks Greek," I had been trying to figure out how today's busy housewives and career girls could accomplish this with a minimum of time and hassle—and without having to resort to the electric can-opener or the assembly-line produced, ready-made dinners.

The thought became a challenge—after all I had won my battle with frayed hostess' nerves by opting the *The One Pot Dinner*—so why not take on Father Time?

I gently but firmly put out of my mind Chaucer's line from *The Canterbury Tales*, "In wicked haste there is no profit"; just as easily I convinced myself that Thomas Shadwell had not had me in mind when he wrote, "The haste of a fool is the slowest thing in the world"; and I totally refused to even consider Robert Louis Stevenson's line, "He sows hurry and reaps indigestion." This was no time for negative thinking.

Instead I sought inspiration and encouragement from such lines as Benjamin Franklin's "Remember that time is money," and John Dryden's positive statement, "They can conquer who believe they can."

I suffered only a temporary relapse of Doubting Thomasitis when a friend remarked that the battle with Father Time was one I would never win. In his estimation I could have been Don Marquis' model for these profound lines from *archy and mehitabel:* "Procrastination is the art of keeping up with yesterday."

For a moment there I saw my hopes for *The Thirty Minute Dinner* go down the drain and I suddenly felt very much like the main character in Mrs. E. Craster's little poem:

> *The centipede was happy quite*
> *Until a toad in fun*
> *Said, "Pray, which leg goes after which?"*
> *That worked her mind to such a pitch,*
> *She lay distracted in a ditch,*
> *Considering how to run.*

But I managed to get out of my self-made ditch and started to work on how to fix a tasty, colorful meal within thirty minutes. I realized I would have to face more than one pot—a momentary traumatic set-back—but found to my relief that in most cases I could keep it down to two. Doing dishes seems to be a hang-up of mine that I trust I share with a lot of others. Wouldn't it be nice if more men heeded the subtle hint furnished by Heywood Broun in "Holding a Baby": "It would be interesting to figure out just how many foot-pounds of energy men have saved themselves, since the creation of the world, by keeping up the pretense that a special knack is required for washing dishes and for dusting, and that the knack is wholly feminine?"

Also, a flood of grandmotherly childhood admonitions started coming back to me, such as "Never leave a room empty-handed," an instruction I incidentally—as a child and to my grandmother's never-ending consternation—took to mean that I should help myself to another piece of fruit or candy from the big silver bowl that to me was the center of the living room. Later in life I realized it is actually a tremendous time saver. And there were others such as "Procrastination is the thief of time," " 'Tis a credit to any good girl to be neat," "An empty belly hears nobody," "Readiness is all," "A grain of prudence is worth a pound of craft," "Spend not where you may save; spare not, where you must spend."

Thus morally armed by a beloved voice out of the past, I went to work.

I think I should reassure you here that I don't have a kitchen filled with all sorts of gadgets—and certainly not an oven that will bake a potato in 4 seconds and roast a side of beef in 35 minutes. I live in a roomy old apartment with enormous closets, the doors of which mysteriously open and close, causing some of my friends to say that a former tenant, Marilyn Monroe, is visiting. However, I am afraid it's just the wind in the air chutes. The building is a marvel of Spanish architecture, the huge patio a joy of well-manicured lawns and hedges, but the kitchens were designed during a period when the tenants were expected to take most of their meals out in glamorous spots. It's therefore very seldom that aromas other than coffee —and instant at that—waft through the stairways. The design of the kitchens has a discouraging effect on cooks less undaunted than me.

I mention this only to convey the idea that all the recipes in this book can not only be fixed in a minimum of time, but also in a minimum of space.

I did learn, however, that the trick in getting dinner ready in thirty minutes is to have all the ingredients and utensils out in plain sight and within easy reach. No matter how well organized your kitchen shelves may be, valuable time is lost in searching for that rarely used herb or spice, or that particular dish you need right now—so please, observe the golden rule whenever you use the book.

I also discovered that social chatter while cooking can be a hindrance. Adopt that Greta Garbo attitude—"I want to be alone"—and repair to the kitchen in solitude. Helpful mates and friends have an absolutely incredible knack for always standing right where you want to be—and furthermore, why should you share the glory with anybody when it's you who are performing the miracle of getting dinner ready in thirty minutes?

Also, in case you think I worked in sanctified peace and quiet, let me hasten to tell you that just about the time I started work on *The Thirty Minute Dinner,* an eight-week-old Pekingese puppy made his appearance in my house. Showing a total disdain for cottage cheese and other puppy goodies, he thrived with avaricious gluttony on the hemlines of slacks and long skirts, so, much of my cooking was done with a little furry appendage dragging along the floor—a cute sight maybe, but certainly not a factor that adds to your mobility or speed. A baby you can put in a crib or high chair, but have you tried to discipline a wiggly puppy who looks at you with unashamed love in his eyes?

During the months of writing this book I also learned what love is—it's friends letting you try out new recipes on them ... and letting a pup chew on their toes. But, more important, I discovered that there are a lot of good and tasty dishes that can be prepared in thirty minutes if you take advantage of your friendly butcher and some of the shortcuts offered today. I can't promise you that you will dance around in the living room while dinner is being made, like that lady in a certain TV commercial, but the book should enable you to live up to Alexander Dumas' definition of dinner: "A major daily activity, which can be accomplished in worthy fashion only by intelligent people. It is not enough to eat. To dine, there must be diversified, calm conversation. It should sparkle with the rubies of the wine between courses, be deliciously suave with the sweetness of dessert, and acquire true profundity with the coffee." And if you feel that Monsieur Dumas should have stuck with his Three Musketeers, let me remind you that it says in the Bible, "Soul, thou hast much goods laid up for many years; take thine ease—eat, drink and be merry."

Or, in the words of Samuel Johnson, "He who does not mind his belly will hardly mind anything else."

SEAFOOD

The famed gourmet Brillat-Savarin once said; "If a shadow of justice remained in this world, cooked crayfish would be the object of divine worship."

As a child I definitely did not share his opinion, but I was brought up at a time when the general rule still was, "A child should be seen and not heard," and these words of Robert Louis Stevenson were oft quoted:

> *A child should always say what's true*
> *And speak when he is spoken to,*
> *And behave mannerly at table;*
> *At least as far as he is able.*

At one point during my childhood I attended a boarding school known for its scholastic record, if not for its culinary finesse. Life there was a never-ending series of rules and regulations, one of which was that boiled codfish was to be served for dinner every Wednesday. I was not fond of codfish and had tried to explain that, as a Pisces, I should not eat my own kind. But astrology was not in vogue then and my pleas fell on deaf ears. I tried as hard as I could to live up to Stevenson's words and behave mannerly at table, but every Wednesday afternoon—which was when we ate dinner—would find me and a by then cold plate of boiled codfish the sole occupants of the dining hall. While the other girls, having dutifully cleared their plates, were out playing, I would sit and stare at the cod as images of a scene depicted by Alexander Dumas more than half a century before flashed through my mind: How the cod's fecundity was equal only to its voracity, and how in large cods up to nine million eggs had been found... eggs that would turn into cod that would all converge on me. And if that wasn't bad enough, Mr. Dumas had further predicted that if nothing was done to prevent the hatching and growing of these cods, one would within three years be able to walk across the Atlantic Ocean on solid codfish. I would have liked to escape, but certainly not that way.

By the time study hall came around, the plate would be removed and it and I would not meet until suppertime —with equally bad results, I may add. Without knowing it I had designed the first diet of fasting one day a week.

I mention this traumatic experience only to prove that if after that you can develop a fondness for seafood—and I have—the dishes have to be good. My fondness almost turned into ecstasy when I discovered how little time is actually needed to come up with tasty dishes based on fish and other seafood—although I must admit you won't find any recipes here using cod.

Trusting that Thomas Jordan meant what I thought he did when he said, "Fish dinners will make a man spring like a flea," here are some recipes that not only seemed to please my male friends, but also passed that acid test of the race against the hands of the clock, a race that brings to mind Benjamin Franklin's words: "Dost thou love life? Then do not squander time, for that's the stuff life is made of."

The Thirty Minute Dinner

This first recipe is so easy and quick that you actually will have time for a drink with your husband or guests. Since all the ingredients fall within the category of staples, it has the further advantage that it can be made on the spur of a rainy moment when marketing becomes a chore ... and most divine of all, it needs only one pot to cook in.

CLAM RISOTTO
(4 Servings)

2 7-oz. cans chopped clams, undrained
1 med. onion, chopped
2 tbsp. butter or margarine
2 tbsp. olive oil
1 1-lb. can tomatoes
1 cup raw rice
1/2 tsp. oregano or dill weed
1 tsp. salt
1/4 tsp. white pepper
Parmesan cheese

Chop the onion while you are heating the butter or margarine with the olive oil in a medium-sized saucepan. Sauté onion in butter mixture for about 5 minutes, under cover, until translucent and limp. Now add the tomatoes, rice, and clams which you have drained into a 2-cup measuring cup. Add enough water to clam liquid to make

1 1/2 cups liquid. Sprinkle salt, pepper, and herbs over rice mixture, pour liquid over, bring to a quick boil, turn heat down, and let simmer for about 20 to 25 minutes.

Serve with a green salad on the side and have some Parmesan cheese on hand for those who like it. All you need for dessert is fresh fruit.

NOTES

This next dish seems to have the characteristics that appeal to men, so if your fellow should eat a little more than his calorie account allows, just remind him he is not the only one to fail. As Oscar Wilde once said: "I couldn't help it. I can resist everything except temptation."

HE-MAN SCALLOPS
(4 Servings)

2 lbs. scallops (thawed out if frozen)
2-3 tbsp. butter or margarine
1 med. onion, diced
1 green pepper, seeded and diced
1 cup light cream
1/4 cup dry sherry
1 tsp. Worcestershire sauce
1 4-oz. can pimiento, drained and diced
1 tbsp. parsley
1/2 tsp. salt
1/4 tsp. white pepper
1 cup crushed potato chips
1/4 cup pine nuts *Optional*
Butter or margarine

Set oven at 450°. In an ovenproof dish melt the butter or margarine and sauté the diced onion and green pepper on top of the stove, under cover, for about 5 minutes, while in a small bowl you mix together the cream, sherry, Worcestershire sauce, diced pimiento, parsley, salt, and pepper. When onion mixture is limp and translucent, remove from heat, arrange scallops on top of this, and pour cream mixture over all. Sprinkle crushed potato chips and pine nuts on top, dot with butter, and bake for 15 minutes.

Serve with hard-crust dinner rolls you heat in the oven with the scallops; sliced tomatoes (Do you know they now come in a can?) marinated in your favorite bottled dressing; and foaming glasses of beer.

Follow this with a cheese tray or—if you want to make a real occasion out of it—and if strawberries are in season, why not try this easy dessert:

STRAWBERRY-BANANA DELIGHT
(4 Servings)

1 box strawberries, washed and hulled
2 bananas, peeled and sliced
1-2 tbsp. sugar
1/2 cup commercial sour cream
1 tsp. grated lemon peel

Stir the sugar and lemon peel, available on your grocer's spice shelf, into the sour cream and gently fold the fruit into this, making sure everything is coated before you put it in the refrigerator to chill until ready to serve.

I assure you these Scallops Supreme live up to their name—but they also require total concentration and application, so grab your Garbo hat, say with conviction; "I want to be alone," go to the kitchen, and get out all the ingredients and a few pots and pans. After dinner you can always drop the Garbo attitude and accept help with the dishes.

It's a rich entree so all you need for dessert is fresh fruit ... that'll also give you time to catch your breath.

SCALLOPS SUPREME
(4-6 Servings)

2 12-oz. pkgs. frozen scallops, thawed
1 1/2 cups dry white wine
2 tbsp. lemon juice
12 large mushrooms, washed and quartered
2 green peppers, seeded and diced
1/4 cup butter or margarine
1/2 tsp. salt
1/4 tsp. white pepper
4 tbsp. flour
1 cup Swiss cheese, grated
1/2 cup Parmesan cheese
1 cup whipping cream, whipped
Paprika
Butter or margarine

Heat the wine and lemon juice to almost boiling point over low heat in a medium-sized saucepan while you wash and quarter the mushrooms and dice the green pepper. Add vegetables together with scallops to wine mixture and let simmer, under cover, for about 8 minutes. While this is simmering, grease either six individual baking dishes or one large one, whip the cream, and grate the Swiss cheese. Just before the simmering time is up, melt the butter or margarine in another medium-sized saucepan, blend in salt, pepper, and flour before gradually adding the liquid in which the scallops and vegetables were cooked. Cook until thickened, about 5 minutes, and if it gets a little lumpy beat it with a wire whisk. Now add the grated Swiss cheese and 1/4 cup of the Parmesan cheese. Stir until melted and well blended, remove from heat, fold in whipped cream, and then gently stir in scallop mixture. Divide among individual baking dishes or gently transfer to the one big baking dish, sprinkle remaining Parmesan cheese on top, dot with a little more butter or margarine, dust with paprika, and run under broiler for 2 to 3 minutes, or until golden brown.

Serve with croissants you have heated in the oven during the last 10 minutes, marinated sliced tomatoes, and, by all means, a bottle of chilled white wine.

The Thirty Minute Dinner

We may use the word "shrimp" disparagingly in referring to someone's size, but mixed with fondness, one would assume, considering the popularity of this crustacean in these United States. This next recipe is a shortcut to the ever-popular Shrimp Curry, but nobody would ever guess.

CURRIED SHRIMP À LA U.S.
(4 Servings)

2 8-oz. pkgs. frozen jumbo shrimp
1 pkg. saffron rice
1 tbsp. butter or margarine
1/4 tsp. caraway seed
1 inner heart of celery, chopped, leaves and all
1/4 lb. butter or margarine
1/3 cup flour
1 1-lb. can apple sauce
1 pkg. onion soup mix
2 cups water
2 chicken bouillon cubes
2-4 tsp. curry powder
1/2-1 tsp. ginger
1/4 cup lemon juice

Start to cook your saffron rice according to package instructions, while you melt 1 tbsp. of butter or margarine in a small skillet. Chop the celery and sauté, sprinkled with caraway seed, under cover for about 5 minutes, while in another medium-sized saucepan you melt the rest of the butter or margarine. To this you add the flour, stirring into a paste. Add the apple sauce, onion soup mix, water, bouillon cubes, curry *to taste*, ginger, lemon juice, and sautéed celery. Heat over medium heat, stirring until thickened. By now the rice should be 10 minutes from being cooked, so add your frozen shrimp to curry mixture and continue simmering for the remaining 10 minutes.

Serve shrimp over rice accompanied by such condiments as raisins, salted peanuts, and toasted coconut chips—all of which just have to be dumped out of their containers into little bowls. Beer makes a nice beverage for this dish and you may follow up with either a cheese tray or fresh fruit.

The Thirty Minute Dinner

This next dish I'm giving to you to serve three because it's the kind of recipe that's ideal for when your husband on short notice brings an important out-of-town business connection home for dinner. If you want to serve more, you just double the quantities — but the personalized touch of the little packets may make your guests think you went to extra special trouble, and in the words of Jonathan Swift:

'Tis an old maxim in the schools,
That flattery's the food of fools;
Yet now and then your men of wit
Will condescend to take a bit.

SHRIMP EN PAPILLOTE
(3 Servings)

9 jumbo shrimp
1 4-oz. can mushroom pieces, drained
1 6-oz. jar Hollandaise sauce
1/2 tsp. dill weed
1/2 tsp. salt
1/4 tsp. white pepper
1 pkg. curried rice

Set your oven at 400° and cook rice according to instructions, while you bring 6 cups of water to a boil for the raw shrimp. Cook shrimp until they turn pink. Discard water and peel and devein shrimp. Now tear off three squares of aluminum foil, about 6 by 6 inches, put three shrimps on each square, divide the drained mushrooms among the three portions, cover with Hollandaise sauce, and sprinkle with dill weed, salt, and pepper before wrapping the foil tightly around each portion. Bake in preheated oven for 10 minutes and serve right out of the packets, with rice on the side and sliced tomatoes, marinated in a good bottled herby oil-and-vinegar dressing.

A bottle of chilled white wine is very good with this, and if you're worried this may not quite satisfy the male appetites, you have time to fix:

CONSOMMÉ AU PORT
(3 Servings)

2 10-oz. cans beef consommé
1/2 cup port wine
1 8-oz. can Julienne carrots
1/4 tsp. caraway seed
Croutons

Pour consommé into small saucepan, add port, carrots, and caraway seed, and bring to a boil. Let simmer for 5 minutes before serving with store-bought croutons on top.

Whether or not you preface the shrimp with the soup, for dessert have a cheese and fruit tray, and your husband's executive ability will only be surpassed by your ingenuity in coming up with a very special dinner on short notice.

The Thirty Minute Dinner

The word "Stroganoff" conjures up visions of creamy, luscious dishes and this next recipe is no different. Should you want to simplify it even more—and since it is rich you might want to omit the rice—this is easily done by serving the Stroganoff over Rice Krispies instead of boiled rice—just make sure it's not the sugar-frosted kind. If you've never used Rice Krispies in this fashion, don't knock it. In the words of Cato, "The wise man does no wrong in changing his habits with time."

SHRIMP STROGANOFF
(3-4 Servings)

- 1 1/2 lbs. raw shrimp, shelled and deveined
- 2 cups water
- 2 chicken bouillon cubes
- 1 tbsp. butter or margarine
- 1 cup raw rice
- 1/2 tsp. salt
- 1/4 tsp. white pepper
- 1/2 tsp. dill weed
- 1/2 cup butter or margarine
- 1 med. onion, chipped fine
- 6-8 large mushrooms, washed and quartered
- 2 tbsp. bottled lemon juice
- 1 tbsp. Worcestershire sauce
- 1-2 tsp. seasoned salt
- 1/4 tsp. pepper
- 1 1/2 cups commercial sour cream

Bring the 2 cups of water to a boil with the bouillon cubes, 1 tbsp. butter or margarine, seasoned salt, pepper, and dill weed. When boiling add the raw rice, reduce heat, and let simmer for 25 minutes, giving it a stir after about 10. While this is going on, melt the 1/2 cup butter or margarine in a large, deep skillet, shell and devein shrimp, and chop the onion. Now sauté the shrimp and onion in melted butter for about 5 minutes. Add the mushrooms you by now have cleaned and quartered, together with the lemon juice and Worcestershire sauce, and continue simmering for another 5 minutes. Stir in sour cream, heat through but do not boil, adjust for salt and pepper, and serve over the rice, accompanied by a green salad if you're so inclined.

A glass of beer is nice with this and all you need for dessert is a cup of coffee and a couple of pieces of your favorite imported bittersweet chocolate.

28 The Thirty Minute Dinner

The Belgians claim the best sole comes from Dieppe, while the British pride themselves on their Dover sole; since these locations are separated by the narrow end of the Channel, I don't think it's an issue for the U.N. to look into. Actually, sole coming from anywhere is good fare—as I hope this next recipe will prove.

BELL PEPPER SOLE
(2-3 Servings)

1 lb. fillets of sole, fresh or thawed
2 med. onions, sliced thin
2 green peppers, seeded and cut in strips
1/3 cup butter or margarine
1/2 tsp. dill weed
1/4 tsp. marjoram
1/4 cup flour
1 tsp. salt
1 tsp. paprika
1/4 tsp. black pepper
1 4-oz. can mushroom pieces, drained
1/3 cup dry sherry or dry white wine
1/3 cup light cream
1 pkg. instant mashed potatoes

Melt the butter or margarine in a deep, heavy skillet while you slice the onions and cut the peppers in strips. Sprinkle dill and marjoram into melted butter, stir in onion and green pepper, and sauté for about 5 minutes under cover. Mix the flour with salt, pepper, and paprika and dip fillets into this, making sure they're well coated on both sides. When the vegetable mix is translucent and limp, transfer with a slotted spoon to a plate, and quickly brown the fish fillets well on both sides, being careful not to break them when you turn them over. A wide spatula is good for this. When the fillets are browned, cover with onion-pepper mixture, sprinkle with drained mushroom pieces, and pour wine combined with cream over all. Lower the heat and let simmer for about 5 minutes while you fix the instant mashed potatoes according to package instructions.

Serve the fish fillets right from the skillet with the potatoes on the side. Coffee and your favorite cookies make a nice dessert.

These next two recipes lend themselves very well to intimate candlelight dinners-a-deux. Whatever points you want to pursue during the meal, these dishes should prove subtle but effective allies unless your fellow turns out to be the kind who quotes Molière, saying: "One must eat to live, and not live to eat"; in which case he's hardly worth holding on to.

FILLET OF SOLE À DEUX
(2 Servings)

1 lb. fillet of sole
1 tbsp. butter or margarine
1 green onion, minced
1/2 tsp. dill weed
1/2 tsp. salt
1/4 tsp. pepper
8 large mushrooms, caps only
1 10-oz. pkg. frozen artichoke hearts, partially defrosted
2/3 cup dry Vermouth *or* dry white wine
1/3 cup water
1 cup heavy cream
1 egg yolk
1/4 cup Parmesan cheese

In a deep skillet melt the butter or margarine, coating the entire bottom with it before adding the fillets; sprinkle minced green onion on top, dust with dill weed, salt, and pepper, arrange mushroom caps and artichoke hearts on top, pour wine and water over all, and cook over low heat for about 12 minutes or until fish is flaky and vegetables heated through. With a spoon remove a little of the fish juice and add to the cream you've mixed with the beaten egg yolk. Pour this on top of fish, sprinkle with Parmesan cheese, and run under broiler until brown. Voila—a dish fit for a king.

Serve with hard-crust dinner rolls and a glass of chilled white wine. Follow this with an assortment of petits fours from your favorite pastry shop and you will truly have lived up to William Cowper's words:

> *If you mean to please*
> *Press your point with modesty and ease.*

FILLET OF SOLE DELICIEUX
(2-3 Servings)

1 lb. fillets of sole (4 in all)
3 1/2 tbsp. butter or margarine
1 tbsp. flour
1/2 tsp. salt
2 tsp. bottled lemon juice
1/4 tsp. prepared horseradish
1/4 tsp. Worcestershire sauce
1 pinch onion powder
1 dash hot pepper sauce
1 dash white pepper
1/3 cup light cream
1 7-oz. can crab meat, picked and flaked
Paprika
1 10-oz. pkg frozen asparagus
1/4 cup Parmesan cheese
1 tbsp. butter or margarine

Pre-heat oven to 350°. In a saucepan melt 1 1/2 tbsp. of the butter or margarine, add the flour and salt together with 1/2 tsp. of the lemon juice, the horseradish, Worcestershire sauce, onion powder, hot pepper sauce, and pepper. Now slowly stir in the light cream and cook until thickened. Remove saucepan from heat and stir in the picked and flaked crab meat. Now grease a shallow baking dish generously, place two of the fish fillets in the bottom, divide the crab mixture between them, and top this with the two remaining fillets. Combine the remaining butter, which you have melted on top of the stove, with the leftover 1 1/2 tsp. lemon juice. Brush fillets with this, dust generously with paprika, and bake for about 20 to 25 minutes, or until fish is flaky. While the fish is baking cook the asparagus according to package instructions, and just before serving drain them and toss with Parmesan cheese and another tbsp. butter or margarine. Have a bottle of chilled white wine ready, together with some hard-crust dinner rolls which you have heated in the oven with the fish during the last 10 minutes.

Since the final baking of the fish might just run you a smidgeon over thirty minutes, you can keep us both honest by serving this tasty soup first!

DANISH CONSOMMÉ
(2-3 Servings)

2 10-oz. cans beef consommé
1/2 cup dry sherry
1 tbsp. tomato paste
1 4-oz. can peas, drained

In a small saucepan combine consommé with the sherry into which you have blended the tomato paste. Bring to a slow boil before adding the drained peas. Heat through and serve right away in delicate soup bowls.

This next recipe might very well be among the winners as far as speed and expedience are concerned—a fact that doesn't surprise me since it was given to me by a woman friend who's in charge of operations for one of the TV networks, operations being a technical term meaning that at the ring of a telephone you can not only dispatch men and equipment to unscheduled destinations, but also let everybody across the country know what's happening. She does this with as much expertise as she whips up dinners.

FILLET OF SOLE SAUTERNE
(2 Servings)

1 lb. fillets of sole
4 tbsp. butter or margarine
1 tbsp. parsley
1/2 tsp. dill weed
1/2 tsp. seasoned salt
1/2 cup dry white wine
1 1-lb. can potatoes
1 tbsp. butter or margarine

Set oven at 375°. In a flat, ovenproof dish with cover melt the butter or margarine on top of stove before you place the fillets in it. Sprinkle with parsley, dill weed, and seasoned salt, pour wine over, cover, and bake for approximately 10 minutes, or until fish is flaky. Meanwhile, melt another tbsp. of butter or margarine in a small saucepan, drain the potatoes and sauté them in this, under cover, for about 5 minutes.

If you feel like serving a salad along with this, you even have time for that by simply shredding some lettuce, mixing it with 1 8-oz. can of peas, drained, and tossing with your favorite bottled oil-and-vinegar dressing.

For dessert simply serve your favorite ice cream, topped with toasted coconut shreds (which you have toasted in the turned-off oven while eating the fish) and a healthy dash of whatever liqueur you may have on hand.

NOTES

This next recipe may not cross the goal line quite as quickly as the previous one, but then it offers you the advantage of having time for a drink with your guests, as well as disproving with éclat Chaucer's words:

> *There is no workman, whatever he be*
> *That may both work well and hastily.*

SOLE-FUL BROCCOLI BAKE
(2-3 Servings)

1 lb. fillets of sole
1 10-oz. pkg. frozen broccoli
1 egg white
1/4 cup mayonnaise
1 green onion, minced
1/4 tsp. Worcestershire sauce

Set oven at 425°. Cook frozen broccoli according to package instructions while you grease an ovenproof dish and beat the egg white until very stiff. (You can mix the yolk with your orange juice the next morning—very healthy.) Fold the mayonnaise, minced green onion, and Worcestershire sauce into the stiff egg white. Drain the broccoli and place in bottom of dish, arrange the fish fillets on top, and spoon egg-white mixture over all. Bake for about 15 minutes and serve with rolls you heat along with the fish, sliced tomatoes marinated in a bottled oil-and-vinegar dressing, and a glass of chilled white wine.

Since you have the time and the oven is going, you may want to wind up dinner with this Danish-inspired dessert:

APPLE-PRUNE BAKE
(2-3 Servings)

1/2 cup cooked, pitted prunes
2 baking apples, cored and
   diced
1/4 cup orange juice
1/4 cup dry sherry
1/4 cup flour
1/4 cup granulated sugar
1/4 cup Cheddar cheese, grated
1/2 cup chopped walnuts
1/2 cup heavy cream, whipped
1/4 tsp. cinnamon

With kitchen scissors snip prunes into bits into a medium-sized bowl, and mix with all other ingredients except cream and cinnamon. Butter a pretty baking dish generously, spoon fruit mixture into this, cover with lid or aluminum foil, and bake in your 425° oven for about 20 to 25 minutes. Serve warm, passing the whipped cream you've flavored with cinnamon. Since this is covered, it's perfectly safe to start it baking while you have the fish in the oven.

38 The Thirty Minute Dinner

As a chubby child I felt very much overshadowed by a very beautiful mother. My best consolation was derived from reading the last verse of Rudyard Kipling's "My Rival":

> *But even she must older grow*
> *And end her dancing days,*
> *She can't go on forever so*
> *At concerts, balls, and plays.*
> *One ray of priceless hope I see*
> *Before my footsteps shine;*
> *Just think, that She'll be eighty-one*
> *When I am forty-nine.*

It was also Kipling who'd given me a stirring, romanticized idea of adulthood:

> *Land of our birth, we pledge to thee*
> *Our love and toil in the years to be;*
> *When we are grown and take our place,*
> *As men and women with our race.*

I envisioned myself as a modern-day Joan of Arc, so imagine my surprise when my first sensation of being treated as an adult came at a charity luncheon hostessed by my mother, when I was asked what I thought my age group could do to help the troops being drafted under the clouds of the oncoming World War II. But to top this off, in spite of braces on my teeth the waiter poured wine for me, and instead of giving me a child's plate put down this next dish in front of me ... a dish that to this time not only remains one of my favorites, but also brings back that long-ago day.

Since it may take just a minute or two over thirty minutes to prepare, I have included a soup in the menu. That way I can have the pleasure of giving you this recipe and still remain true to my thirty-minute pledge.

COQUILLES ST. JACQUES
(4 Servings)

1 lb. scallops, thawed
1/2 lb. fillet of sole
1/2 cup dry sherry
6 tbsp. butter or margarine
1 med. onion, diced
1/4 cup flour
1 1/4 cup light cream
12 large mushrooms, washed and quartered
1 green pepper, seeded and cut in strips
1 tbsp. Worcestershire sauce
1 cup grated Swiss cheese
6 oz. small shrimp, cooked

Set your oven at 350° before you get out one small bowl, a medium-sized saucepan, a small skillet and a 2-qt. ovenproof dish. Put the drained scallops in the small bowl, cut the fillets of sole into bit-size pieces, mix with scallops, and pour sherry over. While you melt 4 tbsp. of the butter or margarine in the medium-sized saucepan, dice your onion and then sauté for about 5 minutes before you add the flour and gradually stir in the light cream. Bring to a boil, stirring all the time, reduce heat, and let simmer for about 10 minutes, while in the skillet you sauté the cleaned mushrooms and green pepper in the remaining butter or margarine, keeping an eye on the sauce. When the 10 minutes are up remove cream sauce from heat, add mushroom-pepper mixture to it together with Worcestershire sauce and grated Swiss cheese, stirring until cheese has melted. Now add the sherry-drenched scallops and sole. Pour into greased baking dish and leave in oven for 15 to 20 minutes or until bubbly. Just before you serve the below listed *Tomato Consommé* that keeps me honest, stir the small, cooked shrimp into the mixture and put some dinner rolls in the oven to heat along.

TOMATO CONSOMMÉ
(4 Servings)

2 10-oz. cans beef consommé
3 6-oz. cans tomato juice
1/4 cup brandy

Pour everything into a small saucepan, heat slowly to boiling point and serve with chives (you can get them all year 'round in the frozen-food department) sprinkled on top.

The Coquilles St. Jacques most definitely deserves a bottle of chilled white wine. It is the kind of dish that brings to mind the words of Robert Louis Stevenson: "The world is so full of a number of things, I think we should all be happy as kings."

NOTES

42   The Thirty Minute Dinner

After a recent trip across the country I realized how lucky we are here in California to have such a variety of produce available to us on a year 'round basis. If avocados are seasonal where you live, promise me to save this recipe for when they're on the market; and even though you may think it has an aura of the ladies' luncheon, let me assure you that it goes over very well with men.

AVOCADO SEAFOOD SHELLS
(4 Servings)

1 10-oz. can cream of celery soup
2 tbsp. lemon juice, bottled
1/4 tsp. dry mustard
1 tsp. prepared horseradish
1 tsp. Worcestershire sauce
1 tsp. instant minced onion
1/2 cup mayonnaise
1 2-oz. can sliced olives, drained
1 12-oz. can whole kernel corn, drained
2 4-oz. cans shrimp
2 avocados, ripe
1/2 cup fine bread crumbs
1/2 cup shredded Cheddar cheese

Set oven at 400°. Mix together in a bowl the celery soup, lemon juice, mustard, horseradish, Worcestershire sauce, minced onion, mayonnaise, and sliced olives, making sure it's all blended. Drain the corn and add, together with the shrimp (cut in pieces if large). Incidentally, if your butcher carries the small, cooked shrimp in packages they're even better for this dish. Cut the avocados in half, remove the pit (this is easily done if you rap the pit first with the edge of a knife), peel the tough skin off, and place in a lightly greased baking dish. Spoon soup-corn-shrimp mixture into and around the avocados, sprinkle bread crumbs and cheese on top, and bake for 15 minutes. Serve with dinner rolls that you heat along with the avocados according to package instructions.

If you're worried that this might not be enough for your more hearty appetites, you have time to fix a soup to serve first, such as this:

PRESTO BORSHT
(4 Servings)

1 1-lb. can Julienne beets, undrained
1 10-oz. can beef consommé
1 tbsp. instant minced onion
1/2 tsp. salt or *to taste*
3 tbsp. bottled lemon juice
1-2 tbsp. brown sugar
1/2 cup beer
Commercial sour cream

Combine all ingredients except sour cream in a medium-sized saucepan; bring to a boil and let simmer for about 15 minutes. Serve piping hot, with dollops of sour cream on top . . . and since you had to open a can of beer, you might as well serve beer throughout this meal . . . everybody will appreciate it.

44   The Thirty Minute Dinner

This next recipe is an absolute boon to the busy housewife since it doesn't even call for anything to be defrosted. Without any fuss you can fix a fish stew that very well may make your guests recall the thought expressed by Julia Carney in "Little Things":

> *Little drops of water, little grains of sand,*
> *Make the mighty ocean and the pleasant land.*
> *So the little moments, humble though they be,*
> *Make the mighty ages of eternity.*

SPEEDY FISH STEW
(4-6 Servings)

1 12-oz. pkg. *each* of frozen
   sole, haddock, and perch
1 9-oz. pkg. frozen lobster tails
1/2 cup olive oil
2-3 med. onions, sliced
3 cloves garlic, *optional*
1 1-lb. can whole carrots, drained
1 1-lb. can tomatoes
1 cup water
1 chicken bouillon cube
1 cup bottled clam juice
1 cup dry white wine
1/2 tsp. crumbled bay leaves
1/2 - 1 tsp. thyme
1/2 - 1 tsp. sweet basil
1/2 - 1 tsp. dill weed
1 tsp. salt or *to taste*
1/2 tsp. white pepper

In a large, heavy pot or kettle—one you can bring right to the table—heat the oil and saute onion and garlic (if you use it) for about 5 minutes, or until limp and translucent. Meanwhile measure out all the other ingredients. Discard the garlic, add the drained carrots, the tomatoes, frozen fish, water, clam juice, and wine together with all the seasonings. Give it a good stir and over medium heat bring to a slow boil. Now add your frozen lobster tails and continue simmering for another 6 to 8 minutes. With a slotted spoon, fish (pardon the pun) the lobster tails out of the stew. Put on your potholder mittens and with a fork remove the meat from the shells. Cut the meat into bite-size pieces, return to stew and carry the pot proudly to the table where you ladle the stew into soup bowls. Have some garlic bread you've heated in the oven ready to pass around along with a jug of chilled white wine.

This is such a sturdy dish that all you'll need for dessert is fresh fruit.

The Thirty Minute Dinner

After reading that Sophia Loren ascribed much of her world-renowned beauty to her daily consumption of spaghetti, I decided to add that Italian pasta to my physical improvement program. Sadly, but truthfully, I must admit that Miss Loren doesn't have to worry about any competition from me, but the program did lead to the discovery of some new ways to use spaghetti, as witnessed by the next two recipes.

CREAMY CLAM SPAGHETTI
(4 Servings)

4 tbsp. butter or margarine
2 7-oz. cans minced clams
1 8-oz. pkg. cream cheese
1 10-oz. can mushroom pieces, drained
1 tsp. dill weed
1/2 tsp. marjoram
1/2 tsp. salt or *to taste*
1/2 tsp. black pepper
1/2 cup Parmesan cheese
1 8-oz. pkg. spaghetti or egg noodles

While the spaghetti or egg noodles are cooking in a large pot according to package instructions, in a smaller pot melt the butter or margarine over low heat, add the herbs and spices, together with the undrained clams, the mushroom pieces, the softened (and/or cut-into-pieces) cream cheese, and the parmesan cheese. Heat, stirring constantly, without ever letting it get to a full boil. When the spaghetti is cooked, drain in collander, return to the large pot, and pour clam sauce over. Stir well and serve right out of the pot, accompanied by sliced tomatoes tossed in a bottled oil-and-vinegar dressing.

When I served this to some friends, one of them exclaimed: "Move over, Alfredo!" Although I've never ascertained who Alfredo is, I prefer to think he's one of the better Italian cooks in town. In any case, this is such a hearty dish all you need afterwards is instant expresso— available at your grocer's in many flavors.

NOTES

PISCEAN SPAGHETTI
(4-6 Servings)

1 7-oz. can crab meat,
   drained and picked
2 7-oz. cans tuna, water-packed,
   drained
2 10-oz. cans whole clams
6 tbsp. butter or margarine
1 tsp. salt
1/4 tsp. white pepper
1 tsp. dill weed
1/2 tsp. dry mustard
1/2 tsp. nutmeg
6 tbsp. flour
2 1/2 cups milk
1 cup light cream
1 8-oz. pkg. spaghetti
Parmesan cheese

In a large pot bring water to boil and cook spaghetti according to package instructions. In a smaller pot melt the butter or margarine while you drain and pick the crab meat and drain the tuna. Into the melted butter now sprinkle salt, pepper, dill, mustard, and nutmeg, blending well before adding the flour. Stir to a paste before gradually adding milk and cream, stirring constantly until sauce thickens. Now add the drained crab and tuna, together with the undrained clams, and let heat through. Drain the cooked spaghetti in a collander, return to its pot, pour seafood sauce over, stir well, and serve with Parmesan cheese on the side and a green salad for color.

Glasses of beer go nicely with this and you can forget about dessert. Nobody will have room for it ... or want it.

This last seafood recipe hails from Greece and I must say they do something to a tuna salad that makes you sit up and take notice. It is, of course, exceptionally good on a hot summer day, but satisfying enough for an all-year meal.

GREEK TUNA SALAD
(3-4 Servings)

1 inner heart of celery, diced
2-3 med. tomatoes, in wedges
1 cucumber, sliced
1 large green pepper, diced
1 med. onion, diced *or*
1 bunch green onions, diced
6-8 radishes, sliced
1 1-lb. can potatoes, drained
2 7-oz. cans tuna, drained
1/2 cup olive oil
1/4 cup white wine vinegar *or*
   bottled lemon juice
1 tsp. salt
1/2 tsp. black pepper
1 tsp. prepared mustard
1 2-oz. can sliced olives, drained

Wash and prepare all your vegetables, put them into a large bowl, and mix with the canned tuna. Make your salad dressing, pour over all, toss and serve with sliced olives sprinkled on top. To keep the Greek motif it's a good idea to have some sourdough French bread and some feta cheese, a Greek cheese you can buy in most grocery stores specializing in imported delicacies.

Serve the salad with beer and have some store-bought cheesecake on hand for your more hungry guests. They probably won't need it, but then you can make use of it some other time.

NOTES

BEEF

In describing a dinner party, John Dryden once wrote: "There was plenty enough, but the dishes were ill-sorted; whole pyramids of sweetmeats, for boys and women; but little of solid meat for men."

And let's face it—the majority of men sympathize with Dryden's feelings because, as it says in the Bible, "Strong meat belongeth to them that are full of age."

However, if after a full day of fighting a variety of problems ranging from suddenly temperamental washing machines to equally impossible bosses, settling an emergency when your five-year-old has lost her favorite teddy bear, or trying desperately to get a twenty-page memo out in an hour before the boss has to catch a plane, you still have to face the role of gracious hostess and get dinner on the table. It may be the straw that can break the camel's back.

Napoleon was only too right when he said to an officer: "You can ask me for anything you like, except time." So . . . start humming the lines from W. S. Gilbert's *Mikado:*

> *My object all sublime*
> *I shall achieve in time—*

and pay heed to the Roman playwright Terrence: "There is nothing so easy but that it becomes difficult when you do it reluctantly."

If after all this pep talk you're still tempted to fix that grand old standby, hamburger, please find the strength to thumb through the following pages and I hope you will find something that will not only intrigue you, but also bring happy smiles to those gathered at your table.

Should you still be wavering, you may get further encouragement from recalling the lines from Longfellow's "The Village Blacksmith":

> *Each morning sees some task begin,*
> *Each evening sees it close;*
> *Something attempted, something done,*
> *Has earned a night's repose.*

But no matter what menu you decide on, do remember what Sir Walter Scott said: "Meat eaten without either mirth or music is ill of digestion."

In referring to the steak, Talleyrand once said: "The United States has thirty-two religions, but only one dish"; ... a somewhat condescending attitude toward a popular food, and I think the French statesman would find few to agree, either then or now.

Since this is such an American dish I find it almost presumptious of me, as an ex-European, to include two recipes on what to do with a steak. I am sure that everybody has their own—and very best—way to fix a steak...but should you still be looking for a favorite way, may I present you with these two inventions of mine:

ROQUEFORT STEAK
(2-3 Servings)

1 1/2 lbs. sirloin steak,
 app. 1 - 1 1/2 in. thick
1 clove garlic, minced
 Salt and pepper *to taste*
1 4-oz. pkg. of Roquefort or
 Blue cheese
1 2-oz. can sliced olives, drained
1 1 lb. can potatoes, drained
1 tbsp. butter or margarine
1 tbsp. parsley

Set oven at broil and let heat up for at least 10 minutes while you lightly brush the broiler rack with oil, tuck half of the minced garlic into strategic spots of the steak and crumble the Roquefort cheese. In due time place the steak on broiler rack 3 to 4 inches from the flame and broil for 5 minutes for rare, turn and sprinkle with remaining garlic, salt and pepper to taste, and continue broiling for another 5 minutes.

Now drain your potatoes, melt the 1 tbsp. butter or margarine in a small saucepan, saute potatoes, under cover, for about 5 minutes before tossing them with the parsley.

Just before you're ready to serve, pull out broiler rack, sprinkle crumbled cheese all over steak, top with sliced olives and return to broiler just until cheese melts.

Serve with a crisp green salad, sparkling with cherry tomatoes. Have a bottle of red wine uncorked, and make it domestic in spite of James Thurber's famous line: "It's a naive domestic Burgundy without any breeding, but I think you'll be amused by its presumption."

If you feel the occasion calls for something special for dessert, you do have time during the first ten minutes to fix the following delicious recipe out of my grandmother's files:

BANANA CREAM WHIP
(3-4 Servings)

3 large, ripe bananas
1 tbsp. dry sherry
2 tsp. bottled lemon juice
1-2 tbsp. sugar
1/2 cup chopped walnuts
1/2 cup heavy cream, whipped

Peel, slice, and mash bananas in medium-sized bowl. Stir in sherry, lemon juice, sugar, and walnuts. Whip the cream in a small bowl (somehow it goes faster that way), and gently fold into banana mixture. Serve in pretty bowl or individual glasses that you keep in the refrigerator until serving time.

DEVILED STEAK
(4 Servings)

1 1 1/2 lbs. sirloin steak,
    app. 1 in. thick
2-3 tbsp. butter or margarine
12 large mushrooms, washed
    and quartered
1 tbsp. parsley
1/2 tsp. marjoram
1-2 tsp. instant onion chips
1 tbsp. dry sherry
1 tsp. Worcestershire sauce
2-3 med. tomatoes, in wedges
1 tbsp. tomato paste
1/2 tsp. sweet basil
1 8-oz. pkg. egg noodles
2 tbsp. butter or margarine
Caraway seed
Salt *To Taste*

Set your oven on broil and let heat up for at least 10 minutes. Start cooking the noodles according to package instructions. Melt the butter in a deep skillet while you wash and quarter the mushrooms; let them sauté in this under cover, sprinkled with parsley, marjoram, and onion chips, for about 5 minutes. Put the steak in the broiler, allowing a total time of 10 to 12 minutes for rare. Add the sherry, Worcestershire sauce, tomato wedges and paste, plus sweet basil to skillet mixture, give it a good stir and let simmer, under cover, until bubbly. By now the noodles should be cooked, so drain them into a colander, return to their pot, and toss with caraway seed and butter. Remove steak from broiler, adjust skillet mixture for salt, and slice steak on carving board at table. Serve the sauce poured over the noodles.

Since this keeps you pretty busy, serve halved avocados with an oil-and-lemon dressing for salad, and just follow this up with Port Salut cheese on toasted dark pumpernickel. A bottle of dry red wine goes nicely with everything.

The following three recipes are all good last-minute company ideas. The Beery Beef Stroganoff may go a little over the alloted 30 minutes so, again, to keep both of us honest, you may want to serve the Presto Borsht from Page 43 first.

The two others have no such limitations, but all three of them will, in the words of Samuel Goldwyn, "include you out" from among those Oliver Wendell Holmes described when he wrote:

> *Among the great whom Heaven has made to shine*
> *How few have learned the arts of arts—to dine.*

BEERY BEEF STROGANOFF
(4 Servings)

1 1/2 lbs. sirloin steak,
   cut in 1/2 in. strips
4 tbsp. butter or margarine
2 med. onions, sliced
4 med. carrots, scraped and
   cut in 1-in. chunks
1 8-oz. can mushroom pieces, drained
1-2 tsp. salt
1/2 tsp. black pepper
1/2 tsp. nutmeg
1/4 tsp. caraway seed
1 tbsp. Worcestershire sauce
1 12-oz. can beer
1 beef bouillon cube
1 cup commercial sour cream
1 pkg. instant mashed potatoes
1/2 tsp. dill weed

While you melt the butter or margarine in a deep, heavy skillet, slice the onions, and let them sauté under cover for about 5 minutes, during which time you cut the meat in strips, prepare the carrots and drain the mushrooms. When onions are limp and translucent, lift them out of skillet with a slotted spoon to a warm platter. Turn heat up under skillet and quickly brown meat. Return the onions to skillet, together with carrots, drained mushrooms, salt, pepper, nutmeg, caraway seed, and Worcestershire sauce. Give it all a good stir before adding bouillon cube and pouring beer over. Cover and let simmer for about 20 minutes. About 5 minutes before you're ready to serve, fix the instant mashed potatoes according to package instructions, adding the dill weed to the liquid—unless you want to try my Rice Krispie trick—see Page 26. Add the sour cream to skillet, heat through but do not boil, and serve all accompanied by foaming glasses of beer.

If you think dessert is in order, just have whatever fresh fruit is in season.

BEEF IN SOUR CREAM
(4 Servings)

1 1/2 lbs. round steak
   cut in thin strips
6 large mushrooms, washed
   and quartered
2-3 tbsp. butter or margarine

1 green pepper, seeded and
   sliced
1 tbsp. instant minced onion
1/2 tsp. thyme
1/4 tsp. marjoram
1 tsp. seasoned salt
1/2 tsp. black pepper
1 can cream of mushroom soup
1 1/2 cups commercial
   sour cream
1 8-oz. pkg. spinach noodles
1 2-oz. can pimiento, diced fine

Cook the spinach noodles according to instructions. Start melting the butter or margarine in a deep skillet while you wash and quarter the mushrooms and slice the green pepper. Sauté vegetables in melted butter, sprinkled with instant onion, thyme, marjoram, seasoned salt, and pepper, under cover, for about 5 minutes, while you slice the meat into strips. With a slotted spoon remove vegetable mixture from skillet to warm platter, add more butter or margarine if necessary, turn up heat, and quickly brown meat. Return vegetables to skillet, reduce heat, and stir in mushroom soup, letting it all heat through until bubbly. By now your noodles should be ready to be drained in a colander. Add more butter in their original pot. Sprinkle pimiento on top and serve right out of the skillet, accompanied by the noodles, glasses of beer, and marinated tomato slices if you like.

This is a hearty dish and all you'll need for dessert is coffee and some of your favorite cookies.

BEEF IN WINE
(4 Servings)

2 lbs. round steak, cut in strips
2-3 tbsp. butter or margarine
8 large mushrooms, washed and quartered
1/2 tsp. marjoram
2 tbsp. tomato ketchup
2 tbsp. soy sauce
2 tsp. meat sauce (Maggi, Bovril, etc.)
5 tbsp. flour
1 14-oz. can beef broth
2 cups dry red wine
1 tsp. crumbled bay leaves
1 1-lb. can onions, drained
1 1-lb. can potatoes, drained
1 tsp. salt
1/4 tsp. black pepper

In a large, deep skillet melt the butter or margarine while you wash and quarter the mushrooms. Let them sauté in this under cover, for about 5 minutes, sprinkled with marjoram, while you cut your meat in strips. With a slotted spoon remove mushrooms to a warm platter, turn heat up, and quickly brown your meat, adding more butter if necessary. Return mushrooms to skillet, reduce heat, and let simmer while you make a paste of the tomato ketchup, soy sauce, meat sauce, and flour. Stir this into meat mixture before adding beef broth, wine, and crumbled bay leaves. Let simmer for about 10 minutes, before adding the drained onions and potatoes, salt and pepper, continue simmering for another 10 minutes, during which you can quickly toss some packaged cole slaw with a bottled oil-and-vinegar dressing.

Serve right from the skillet with a jug of red wine on the side table and also some crusty bread for those who like to sop up the juices.

NOTES

The next two recipes are truly pleasing to male palates, the kind of food that may make your fellow think that in spite of Women's Lib you have started to live according to the words from one of Shakespeare's sonnets:

> *Being your slave, what should I do but tend*
> *Upon the hours and times of your desire?*
> *I have no precious time at all to spend,*
> *Nor services to do, till you require.*

BEEF AND CAULIFLOWER SKILLET
(3-4 Servings)

1 lb. flank steak, in strips
2 tbsp. butter or margarine
1 small cauliflower, in flowerettes
2 tbsp. olive oil
1/4 cup water
1 10-oz. can consomme
1 1/2 tbsp. cornstarch
2 tbsp. soy sauce
2 tbsp. lemon juice
2 tsp. instant minced onion
1 10-oz. pkg. frozen peas
1 tsp. salt
1 2-oz. can shoestring potatoes

Get two skillets out—one large one with cover, one smaller. Wash the cauliflower and with a sharp knife separate into flowerettes; cut the flank steak diagonally into thin strips. In the smaller skillet melt the 2 tbsp. butter or margarine and brown your meat strips in this, while in the larger skillet you heat the 2 tbsp. olive oil and sauté the cauliflower for 3 minutes, turning constantly to prevent browning. Reduce heat, add the 1/4 cup water to the cauliflower, and cover to let steam for another 3 minutes. Keep an eye on the meat strips so they don't burn. While the cauliflower is steaming, mix together in a small bowl consommé, cornstarch, soy sauce, lemon juice, and instant onion. Pour this over cauliflower, together with the meat and its drippings and the frozen peas. Stir everything well, adjust for salt, and cook over medium heat until steaming hot and the peas are heated through.

Serve with shoestring potatoes on the side, either directly from the can, or heated in a 350° oven for about 5 minutes...but I should warn you here: they're pretty salty, so go easy on the salt in the skillet—you can always add more at the table. Those handy sliced tomatoes marinated in bottled dressing taste and look very well with this, as does a glass of ale.

Should you have some leftover meat in the refrigerator, you may substitute this for the flank steak, but please don't try and use frozen cauliflower. Somehow the nutty flavor from the fresh vegetable eludes you when frozen . . . and that is one of the charms of this dish.

SKILLET FLANK STEAK
(2-3 Servings)

1 lb. flank steak, in strips
2-3 tbsp. butter or margarine
1 large onion, chopped
1 large green pepper, seeded and diced
2 large tomatoes, in wedges
1 tsp. seasoned salt
1/2 tsp. black pepper
1/2 tsp. thyme
1/2 tsp. caraway seed
1 2-oz. can sliced olives, drained
1/4 cup brandy
1 beef bouillon cube

While the butter or margarine is melting in a deep skillet, chop your onion and dice the pepper before letting them sauté for about 5 minutes in skillet, under cover. During this, cut your meat into thin diagonal strips and wash and cut tomatoes into wedges. Lift onion mixture out of skillet with slotted spoon to warm platter, increase heat, and quickly brown meat strips, adding more butter or margarine as necessary. Sprinkle meat with seasoned salt and pepper, return vegetable mixture and sprinkle with thyme and caraway seed, adding all other ingredients, give the mixture a good stir, reduce heat, and let simmer for about 15 to 20 minutes. Serve with hard-crust rolls for those delectable juices and have a cheese tray ready as dessert.

A stew has always been synonymous with hours of simmering, right? Wrong. Within 30 minutes it is possible to come up with a dish that has all the beloved attributes of the long-simmering stew—a dish that will make your family once more prove the truth of Victor Hugo's statement: "The supreme happiness of life is the conviction that we are loved."

ROUND STEAK STEW
(3-4 Servings)

1 lb. round steak, in 1-in. pieces
2 tbsp. olive oil
1 pkg. onion gravy mix
1 6-oz. can tomato paste
3/4 cup dry red wine
1/4 tsp. caraway seed
1/2 tsp. dill weed
1 tsp. salt
1/2 tsp. black pepper
1 1-lb. can potatoes, drained with
1 1-lb. can green beans, to make 3/4 cup liquid

While the olive oil is heating in a medium-sized saucepan or deep skillet, cut your meat into 1-1 in. pieces and brown quickly on both sides. While the meat is browning, open your canned vegetables, measuring liquid from them to 3/4 cup, adding water or wine if necessary. Open the tomato paste and gravy mix. When meat is browned, stir in gravy mix, tomato paste, vegetable liquid, wine, caraway seed, and dill, together with salt and pepper. Bring to a boil, reduce heat, and let simmer for about 15 minutes before you add the drained potatoes and beans; continue simmering for another 5 to 10 minutes while you heat some rolls in the oven.

A piece of cheesecake makes a nice dessert for this stew.

NOTES

For some inexplicable, but certainly not justifiable reason, chipped beef seems to have vanished from the American dinner table. So to remedy this tragic situation go to your grocer's delicatessen department, pick up some packages of chipped beef languishing there and elevate this tasty meat to its proper status. After serving this next dish you may find you have lived up to the advice Brillat-Savarin once gave his cook: "Continue to take the greatest care with everything you do, and never forget that once guests have set foot in my parlor, it is our duty to care for their happiness."

CREAMY, DREAMY CHIPPED BEEF
(2-3 Servings)

1/2 lb. chipped beef
1 small onion
1/4 lb. butter or margarine
8 large mushrooms, washed and quartered
3 tbsp. flour
3/4 cup light cream
1/4 cup dry white wine
1/4 tsp. caraway seed
1 cup grated Cheddar cheese
1 cup commercial sour cream
1/2 8-oz. pkg. egg noodles
Parsley

Start by getting out one large pot, one medium-sized pot, and a small skillet. Start cooking the noodles as per package instructions in the large pot. Mince the onion and

70 The Thirty Minute Dinner

the chipped beef—or tear the meat into pieces, whichever goes faster for you. Melt about 6 tbsp. of your butter or margarine in the medium-sized pot and sauté, under cover, the onion and chipped beef for about 5 minutes, or until onion is translucent. Start washing and slicing your mushrooms while the remaining butter melts in the small skillet. Sauté your mushrooms in this for about 5 minutes or until you're ready to use them. To the limp onion-beef mixture, add the flour, stir around, then gradually add your cream, and wine, stirring until sauce is thick and smooth. By now your noodles should be almost ready to be drained. Add the sauteed mushrooms to your large skillet, along with the caraway seed, and let simmer until minutes before you're ready to serve; then add the grated cheese and sour cream, letting it just heat through while you drain the noodles and toss them in their pot with a dot of butter. Serve chipped beef over noodles and garnish with parsley.

Have frosty glasses of beer and dill pickles for those who like them. For dessert all you need is fresh fruit.

When you live in California it is almost impossible not to get involved at one time or another in an argument about the various merits of San Francisco versus Los Angeles. After a visit to both cities a European reporter friend of mine wrote an article in which he compared San Francisco to a middle-aged man, bulging at the waistline and living in the past; whereas he saw Los Angeles as a young man, running off in all directions, not quite certain which one to follow . . . San Francisco eating for pleasure, Los Angeles for energy. After being ostracized for what seemed an endless period of time, I have just been re-accepted into the good graces of my San Francisco friends, an occasion that resulted in the next recipe. Without wanting to get further involved in this California problem, I offer the dish to you with the assurance that no matter where you live or hail from . . . the dish is tasty.

BEEFY SPINACH SKILLET DINNER
(4-6 Servings)

1 1/2 lbs. ground sirloin
1 1-lb. can shopped spinach, well drained
6-8 large mushrooms, washed and qauartered
1 large onion, chopped
2 tbsp. butter or margarine
1/4 tsp. marjoram
1 tsp. salt
1/4 tsp. white pepper
4 tbsp. butter or margarine
6 eggs
1 cup cottage cheese
1/4 tsp. nutmeg
Cayenne

Drain the canned spinach in a colander. Get out one large and one small skillet. Wash and quarter the mushrooms, chop the onions. Melt 2 tbsp. butter or margarine in the small skillet and sauté under cover the mushrooms sprinkled with marjoram, for about 5 minutes. In the large skillet melt the 4 tbsp. butter or margarine and sauté your chopped onion and ground meat, broken up, and sprinkled with salt and pepper until onion is translucent and the meat has lost its pink color. Beat the eggs in a small bowl with the cottage cheese and nutmeg. Stir the sautéed mushrooms into meat mixture, add the drained spinach, let heat through before you add the egg-cottage cheese mixture. Stir easily with wooden spoon until eggs have reached the desired doneness...for me that's 3 minutes. Sprinkle some cayenne on top for color and serve right out of the skillet with sourdough bread and sweet butter. Beer makes a nice beverage, and if you feel like salad, make it sliced tomatoes in an oil-and-vinegar dressing.

This is such a hearty dish that all you will need afterwards is a cup of good, strong coffee and a bite of your favorite chocolate.

The next two recipes are what I call *en famille* recipes ... the kind that lend themselves to a compromise at the time when the kids are clamoring for plain hamburgers and you want something a little more sophisticated.

I am very much aware that Emerson once said, "Every compromise was surrender and invited new demands"; but hope you will find the words of Samuel Johnson,"Life cannot subsist in society but by reciprocal concessions," more applicable to your family.

CHEESY BEEF AND NOODLES
(4 Servings)

1 8-oz. pkg. egg noodles
1 lb. ground beef
1-2 tbsp. butter or margarine
1 med. onion, chopped
1 green pepper, diced
1/2 tsp. oregano
1/2 tsp. thyme
1 tsp. seasoned salt
1/2 tsp. black pepper
1 8-oz. can mushroom pieces, drained
2 8-oz. cans tomato sauce
1/2 lb. Cheddar cheese, grated
1/4 cup commercial sour cream
1 cup cottage cheese

Set oven at 375° and start cooking noodles according to package instructions. Melt 1 tbsp. butter or margarine in a deep skillet while you chop the onion and dice the green pepper. Sauté for about 5 minutes, under cover, before you add the meat, letting that cook until it loses its pink color. Sprinkle with herbs, add the drained mushrooms and tomato sauce, stir, and let simmer while you combine the grated Cheddar cheese with sour cream and cottage cheese in a small bowl. Grease a 2-qt. baking dish with the remaining butter. By now the noodles should be cooked. Drain noodles, mix well with meat and cheese mixtures, using the pot you cooked the noodles in—wipe your brow, and pour everything into baking dish, cover, and let bake for 15 minutes . . . during which you can either have a well-deserved drink, set the table, or explain to the kids why you didn't want to fix hamburgers.

HAMBURGER-VEGETABLE CASSEROLE
(4 Servings)

1 lb. ground beef
1 tbsp. butter or margarine
4 stalks celery, diced
1 med. onion, chopped
1 10-oz. pkg. frozen peas
1 10-oz. can cream of mushroom soup
2 tbsp. milk
2 tbsp. soy sauce
1/2 tsp. black pepper
1 tsp. salt
1 cup crushed potato chips

Set oven at 375°. While you melt the butter and brown the meat in a 2-qt. ovenproof dish, stirring occasionally, dice the celery and chop the onion. When the meat has lost its pink color, stir in the diced celery and frozen peas, and let simmer while you mix together in a small bowl the chopped onion, mushroom soup, milk, soy sauce, salt, and pepper. Pour this over mixture in baking dish, spread crushed potato chips on top, dot with butter, and bake for 20 minutes, under cover, unless toward the end you find it's getting too juicy.

Since this is neither as concerted an effort as the previous one, nor as hearty . . . and since you've got the oven turned on . . . you might want to try and make this dessert with it. It takes its inspiration from the Danish "Kransekage," an absolute delight of ground almonds, sugar, and egg whites . . . but this is a somewhat more calorie-conscious version, although that's difficult when you deal with Danish food.

ALMOND-APPLESAUCE BAKE
(4-6 Servings)

1 1-lb. jar applesauce
1-2 tsp. cinnamon
1 1/2 cups blanched almonds, ground
3 eggs, separated
1-2 tbsp. powdered sugar

Set oven between 375° and 400°. Whir almonds in blender for about 10 seconds. Butter a pretty baking dish. Stir the cinnamon into the applesauce before pouring into baking dish. In a small bowl mix ground almonds with sugar before adding egg yolks one at a time. If you feel the mixture is a little too stiff add a little dry sherry or water. In another bowl, beat the egg whites until very stiff before gently folding almond mixture into whites. Spoon over applesauce and bake for about 20-25 minutes, letting the dish finish while you eat the first course. Serve warm.

When I was growing up in Europe, Ernest Hemingway and A. A. Milne were my literary idols—a combination that always confused my teachers who couldn't see what bull fighters and Winnie the Pooh had in common. I was certain that should I ever come face to face with either, my emotions would be like those experienced by Don Juan through Lord Byron . . . and with a slight paraphrasing of the gender:

> *His overpowering presence made you feel*
> *It would not be idolatry to kneel.*

I never did meet either Mr. Hemingway or Mr. Milne, so I don't know if I would have reacted that way . . . but I do know that upon tasting this next recipe, which owes its origin to Mr. Hemingway, he inched forward in my admiration—after all Mr. Milne had only given me instructions on how to store Pooh honey.

ERNEST HEMINGWAY'S PICADILLO
(4 Servings)

    2 cups water
    3 beef bouillon cubes
    3 tbsp. butter or margarine
    1 med. onion, chopped
    1/4 tsp. garlic powder
    1 cup raw rice
    1/2 cup seedless raisins, soaked
    1 lb. ground beef
    1 tsp. salt
    1/2 tsp. black pepper
    1/2 tsp. marjoram
    1/2 tsp. oregano
    1/2 cup dry wine
    1 cup chopped fresh peaches
    1 stalk celery, sliced
    1 2-oz. can sliced olives, drained
    1/2 cup blanched almonds

While you're waiting for the 2 cups of water to boil in a medium-sized saucepan, to which you've added 2 of the bouillon cubes and 1 tbsp. butter or margarine, melt the other 2 tbsp. butter or margarine in a deep skillet and chop the onion. Sauté onion in butter, sprinkled with garlic powder, for about 5 minutes. As soon as your water boils, add the 1 cup of raw rice, reduce heat, and let simmer for about 25 minutes, under cover, giving it a stir after about 15 minutes.

Now, cover the raisins with water in a separate dish and add the broken-up ground beef to your onion in the skillet, together with salt, pepper, marjoram, and oregano. Cook until it loses its red color, add the wine and the remaining bouillon cube, reduce heat, and let simmer, under cover for about 15 minutes, during which you stir your rice, chop the peaches, slice the celery, and drain the olives. About 5 minutes before you're ready to serve, add all that and the drained raisins to your meat mixture and let just heat through. At serving time pile rice in middle of plate, heap meat mixture on top, and sprinkle with almonds.

To stay with the Hemingway image, instead of dessert why not serve:

RUMMY COFFEE
(1 Serving)

1 cup strong, black coffee
1 tsp. sugar
1/4 cup rum
Whipped cream

Stir sugar and rum into coffee, float whipped cream on top, and serve.

NOTES

The next recipe was intended to bring a little glow to the kind of day Thomas Hood described so well in his poem:

No warmth, no cheerfulness, no healthful ease,
No comfortable feel in any member—
No shade, no shine, no butterflies, no bees
No fruits, no flowers, no leaves, no birds
November!

Not only may the dish restore your faith in better days to come, you may also be lucky enough to have everything on hand, thus making it unnecessary to brave the elements.

PANTRY STEW
(4 Servings)

1 lb. ground beef
2 tbsp. butter or margarine
1 12-oz. can of beer
1 cup water
2 beef bouillon cubes
1 1-oz. pkg. onion gravy mix
1 tsp. salt
1/2 tsp. black pepper
1 tsp. chili powder
1 tbsp. imitation bacon bits
1 small green pepper diced
1 1-lb. can of potatoes, drained
1 8-oz. can whole kernel corn, drained
1 8-oz. can red kidney beans, drained

In a large pot melt the butter or margarine and brown the broken-up meat in this until it loses its pink color.

Add all the other ingredients, stir, bring to a boil, reduce heat, and let simmer for 20 minutes . . . that's all.

Have hard-crust rolls on hand for sopping up juices, and fresh fruit for dessert, unless you want to try this easy and homey dessert:

SKILLET APPLES
(4 Servings)

1 1-lb. can pie apple slices
3 tbsp. butter or margarine
1/4 cup sugar
1/4 cup dry sherry
1/2 cup heavy cream, whipped
1 tsp. cinnamon

Melt butter in a small skillet, lightly brown apple slices, sprinkled with sugar, before pouring sherry over. Let it heat through and serve with whipped cream, flavored with cinnamon. You can fix this either just before you sit down to eat and just keep it warm over the lowest flame possible, or you can do it while some angel clears the table. Either way it is the kind of little touch that makes you think of Robert Louis Stevenson's line:

> *There is no duty we so much underrate*
> *As the duty of being happy.*

The Thirty Minute Dinner

Aside from appealing to the tastes of all ages, this next recipe has the added advantage of being so inexpensive that you can splurge on steaks later in the week. It's this kind of logic that keeps me from ever saving up any money out of the food budget . . . but it does keep the puppy in bones.

PESKY BEEF AND MACARONI
(4-Servings)

1 lb. ground beef
1 8-oz. pkg. elbow macaroni
2-3 tbsp. butter or margarine
12 green onions, diced, tops and all
1 1-lb. can stewed tomatoes
2/3 cup red chili sauce
1 2-oz. can sliced olives, drained
1 tsp. seasoned salt
1/2 tsp. black pepper
1 cup shredded Cheddar cheese

Set the oven at 375°. While you cook the elbow macaroni according to package instructions, melt the butter or margarine in a deep heavy skillet, dice the green onions, and let them saute in this for about 5 minutes, under cover. Add the ground beef, broken up, and sprinkled with salt and pepper and continue cooking until it's lost the red color. Grease a 2-qt. baking dish. Add the stewed tomatoes, chili sauce, and drained olives to meat mixture. Let it heat through. By now your macaroni should be cooked, so you can drain it into a colander before you pour half the meat mixture into the baking dish, cover with half the macaroni, and sprinkle half the grated cheese on top of this. Repeat layers, dot with a little extra butter or margarine, and bake for 15 minutes. Serve with a green salad, and have fresh fruit for dessert.

NOTES

84 The Thirty Minute Dinner

Never having been quite able to shake away the poignant truth of Philip J. Bailey's line, "The sole equality on earth is death," but without wanting to go into the controversy surrounding Women's Lib, I do want to go on record saying that among the many young married couples I know, husband and wife seem to share and share alike, be it in breadwinning or household chores. I have yet to find a wife who agrees with a Mrs. Gaskell who said, "A man is so in the way in the house." Many more hum the line, "It's so nice to have a man around the house."

Maybe today's young husbands are spurred on by Robert Burton's words: "Cookery is become an art, a noble science; cooks are gentlemen"; anyway, it's not unusual today to see the husband in the kitchen while the wife attends to other chores . . . and more power to both. After all, the famed cooks of history were all male, perchance because women were not accepted as historians. In any case, this next recipe comes from such a couple. The husband usually attends to the main course, while the wife is in charge of desserts . . . a department she handles well as witnessed by the date pudding I have included on Page 159.

HAMBURGER PIES À LA LARRY
(3 Servings)

6 packaged hamburger patties *or*
1 1/2 lbs. ground beef
1 tbsp. butter or margarine
1 4-oz. can mushroom pieces, drained
1/3 cup vin rosé

2 tbsp. grated cheese (Cheddar,
  Swiss, or Jack)
1 tsp. seasoned salt
2 8-oz. cans tomato sauce
1 4-oz. can sliced, ripe olives, drained
1/4 tsp. sweet basil
1 dash hot pepper sauce
1/8 tsp. garlic powder
1 pkg. brown rice

If your butcher carries the prepared hamburger patties, get those; otherwise shape the ground beef into 6 large, fairly thin patties. Prepare the brown rice according to package instructions and while the butter or margarine is melting in a large, deep skillet, distribute half the drained mushroom pieces among three of the patties, sprinkle grated cheese on top of this, and pour a little of the wine over before you top with the three remaining patties. Seal the edges very well with your fingers, sprinkle pies with seasoned salt, and brown well in butter or margarine on both sides. Be careful in turning them over—two spatulas will do the trick neatly. When brown pour tomato sauce over the pies, together with the rest of the wine, the remaining mushrooms, the sliced olives, sweet basil, garlic powder, and hot pepper sauce. Stir gently, making sure pies are covered but being careful not to break them. Bring to a slight boil, reduce heat, and simmer, uncovered, for 15 minutes or until your rice is done.

Serve pies on a bed of rice, with sauce poured over, and a green salad on the side, Of course, a glass of vin rosé is not a bad accompaniment, but you really won't need dessert . . . just coffee.

If your knowledge of Denmark is limited to the oft-quoted line from Shakespear's *Hamlet*, "Something is rotten in the state of Denmark"; and Rudyard Kipling's poem:

> *And that is called paying the Dane-geld;*
> *But we've proved it again and again,*
> *If once you have paid him the Dane-geld*
> *You never get rid of the Dane*

you are laboring under a misconception. Denmark is—among other things—Hans Christian Andersen, nonmelancholy Danes who don't pop in and out of bed with each other all the time, marvelous architecture and designs, a lousy climate, and wonderful food.

One of their national dishes is the "Frikadelle"—a meat patty that deserves as much popularity as that enjoyed by its Swedish and Italian cousins. It goes without saying it should be accompanied by the Danish national drink, beer ... and if you think I'm kidding about beer being the national drink, when you call in professional movers in Denmark you're supposed to supply them with a case of beer in addition to their wages ... and in Denmark a case holds 24 bottles of beer! But back to the matter at hand:

FRIKADELLER—DANISH MEAT PATTIES
(4 Servings)

1 lb. ground beef
1 lb. ground pork
1 tbsp. instant minced onion

6 tbsp. flour
1/2 tsp. ground cloves
1/4 tsp. allspice
1/2 tsp. salt or *to taste*
1 1/2-2 cups milk
2 eggs, well beaten
12 tbsp. butter or margarine
2 1-lb. cans potatoes, drained
Parsley
Pickled beets

Have the butcher run the meat through the grinder twice. In a large bowl mix the meats with instant minced onion, flour, cloves, allspice, and salt. Gradually stir in the milk, beating well after each addition. Now add the two beaten eggs and continue stirring until mixture is fluffy and light, and your butter or margarine has melted in a deep large skillet. Drop a large tablespoonful of meat mixture into melted butter and brown well on both sides. If the spoon gets a little sticky and you have difficulties making the meat slip after a few "drops," dip it in the melted butter and you'll have no problems. Reduce heat and let "Frikadeller" simmer for about 15 minutes, during which time you can set the table and sauté the drained potatoes in a little butter or margarine, before you toss them with parsley. Serve the "Frikadeller" right from the skillet; have pickled beets as a salad if you want to stay with Danish tradition, plus the aforementioned beer.

Should you have any left over they're excellent cold for sandwiches.

88   The Thirty Minute Dinner

To give the dessert a Danish flavor start out by fixing this:

DANISH JELLO
(4 Servings)

1 3-oz. pkg. Strawberry Jello
1 cup dry white wine
8 ice cubes
Whipped cream—*optional*

Follow "Speed Set" directions on package, substitute white wine for water. Serve with whipped cream on top since no self-respecting Dane would consider having dessert without this condiment. Incidentally, since the alcoholic content evaporates during boiling, it's perfectly safe to serve this version to children.

I know the ingredients for this next recipe don't look like much, but don't let that fool you. Aside from being an incredibly quick dish it's also very tasty... and economical, which may induce you to try the dessert I have included. If you do, start dinner by fixing the dessert first, then the curry, and you will see Shakespeare's line, "The spirit of time shall teach me speed," come true.

HURRY-UP LEFTOVER CURRY
(4 Servings)

1 large onion, sliced thin
1/2 cup butter or margarine
2-4 tsp. curry
2 tbsp. imitation bacon bits
1/4 cup vinegar
1/4 cup water
1 beef bouillon cube
1 8-oz. can tomato sauce
2 cups leftover beef, diced
1 pkg. instant rice
Green onions
Raisins
Salted peanuts

In a deep skillet melt the butter or margarine—I know it's a lot, but it's right—and sauté the sliced onion for about 5 minutes. Mix the curry and the bouillon cube with the vinegar and water, sprinkle bacon bits over onion, pour curry mixture into skillet, and stir in tomato sauce. Let this simmer for about 5 minutes. Now cook the instant rice according to instructions and add the diced leftover meat to the skillet, letting it heat through before you serve over rice, with little bowls of raisins, peanuts, and chopped green onions as condiments.

If you feel the family deserves a treat, here is the recipe for:

NUT BARS
(2 Dozen)

3 eggs
2 cups light brown sugar
1/2 cup *plus* 2 tbsp. flour
1/8 tsp. salt
1 tsp. vanilla extract
1 cup pecans, crushed

Set the oven at 350° and grease and flour two 8-in. cake pans. Beat the eggs well, add brown sugar, stir until well blended, then add flour, salt, vanilla, and continue stirring. Either whir the pecans in the blender for about 10 seconds or put in a small plastic bag and crush with a rolling pin or empty bottle. Stir into sugar mixture, blend well, and divide between the two pans. Bake for about 20 to 25 minutes. By the time you have finished the first course the cakes will have cooled off enough so you can cut them either into wedges or bars and serve warm with coffee.

NOTES

92 The Thirty Minute Dinner

John Barrymore is quoted as having once said: "The only way to fight a woman is with your hat. Grab it and run." Believe you me, if you serve either of the two meat loaf recipes following, you will have just the opposite problem. Everybody will want to stay around. Both are quite different from the standard meat loaves—good enough for company—and should you have any left over, which I honestly doubt, it is fine for sandwiches as well.

PEANUTTY MINI-MEAT LOAVES
(4-6 Servings)

2 lbs. ground sirloin
1 med. onion, finely chopped
1/2 cup peanuts, finely ground
2 small cans evaporated milk
1 tsp. powdered ginger
1 tsp. turmeric
1 tsp. dry mustard
1/2 tsp. black pepper
1 tbsp. Worcestershire sauce
1/4 cup tomato ketchup
1 pkg. instant mashed potatoes

Set oven at 350°. In blender grind peanuts to a mealy texture. Grease generously a large square or oblong ovenproof dish. In a large bowl mix the onion you have chopped with all other ingredients, except ketchup and instant mashed potatoes. Knead it well with both hands so everything is well blended. Shape into two or three mini-loaves, depending on shape of your dish and bake for 20 to 25 minutes, drizzled with the tomato ketchup. Serve with mashed potatoes you've made according to package instructions during the last 5 minutes of the baking time and a crisp green salad. A glass of beer goes nicely with this and all you need for dessert is fresh fruit.

One more thing . . . don't worry about the different color of this meat loaf as compared to others . . . your eyes are not deceiving you . . . the turmeric gives it a nice dark amber shade . . . and it is correct. No salt is needed.

SPECIAL MINI-MEAT LOAVES
(4-6 Servings)

1 lb. ground beef
1 lb. sausage meat
3/4 cup cottage cheese
1/2 cup sour cream
2 slices rye bread, crumbled
   (delicatessen-style is best)
2 eggs, beaten
1 pkg. onion soup mix
1 tsp. A-1 Sauce
1 tbsp. Worcestershire sauce
1/2 tsp. curry powder
1/2 tsp. nutmeg
1/4 tsp. ginger
1-2 tsp. salt
1/4 tsp. white pepper
1 pkg. instant mashed potatoes

Set oven at 350° and grease a large ovenproof dish well. Mix all ingredients except the mashed potatoes with your hands in a big bowl, making sure everything is kneaded well. Shape into three or four mini-loaves, depending on the shape of your dish, place in baking dish, dot with additional butter or margarine on top, and bake for 20 to 25 minutes. During the last 5 minutes fix your instant mashed potatoes as per package instructions and serve to some lucky guests with foaming glasses of beer and dill pickles on the side.

If you really want to shine, why not serve for dessert:

FLAMING STRAWBERRIES
(4-6 Servings)

2 boxes strawberries, washed and hulled
2 tsp. orange peel
1 tsp. lemon peel
8 tsp. sugar
1/2 cup brandy

Before you start worrying about the orange and lemon peel let me assure you, you should use the kind available in jars on your grocer's spice shelf. Now wash and hull the strawberries and arrange in a pretty dish. In a small saucepan heat the brandy with sugar, orange, and lemon peel, turn off heat, ignite and pour over strawberries . . . an easy but very special dessert. Incidentally, always remember to turn off your source of heat before you ignite any of your flaming recipes.

Henry S. Canby once said: "Style is like happiness. Everyone recognizes it, everyone describes it, but no two people agree as to its exact nature." This statement applies equally well to tastes in food. In the next recipe, however, I hope you will find so many of the elements more than two people can agree upon as favorites that it will turn into a regular crowd pleaser for you.

MEATBALL STEW
(4 Servings)

1 lb. ground beef
1/2 cup dry bread crumbs
1 egg, beaten
1/4 cup tomato sauce
1 tsp. salt
1/4 tsp. black pepper
1/4 tsp. allspice
1-2 tsp. instant minced onion
2-3 tbsp. butter or margarine
3/4 cup tomato sauce
1 cup dry red wine
1 pkg. onion soup mix
2-3 large carrots, pared and sliced
1 10-oz. pkg. frozen peas
1 1-lb. can potatoes, drained

In a large bowl blend ground beef with bread crumbs, the beaten egg, the 1/4 cup tomato sauce, salt, pepper, allspice, and instant onion. When all is well blended and there's no better way than using your hands, melt butter or margarine in a large, deep skillet, shape meat mixture into 12 balls, and brown these well on all sides. Add all other ingredients, except potatoes, bring to a boil, then reduce heat, and let simmer for 15 minutes under cover, adding the drained potatoes during the last 5 minutes. Serve with rye bread, sweet butter and beer and have a quick-cooking tapioca pudding for dessert.

NOTES

William Cowper once said:

> *Variety's the very spice of life*
> *That gives it all its flavour.*

So to further prove the point earlier made that there is a meatball world outside Italy and Sweden, let me illustrate it by the following six recipes. The only thing they have in common is that they may all be called meatballs . . . everything else about them is as different as their points of origin.

The first recipe requires not only several saucepans, but also your undivided attention. Should you feel slightly put upon after thirty minutes of toil, just remember the words of Kahlil Gibran: "Work is love made visible"; and you'll feel a lot better.

HUNGARIAN MEATBALLS
(4-6 Servings)

1 1/2 lb. ground sirloin
1 cup dry bread crumbs
1 cup milk
1 small onion, finely diced *or*
1-2 tsp. instant minced onion
1 tsp. salt
1/4 tsp. hot pepper sauce
1/4 tsp. marjoram
1/4 tsp. tarragon
2 tbsp. flour
1 tbsp. paprika
2 cups sour cream
1 8-oz. pkg. noodles
1 - 2 tbsp. butter or margarine
Poppy seed

Fill a medium-sized saucepan half-full of water, lightly salted, and bring to a boil, while in a bowl you break up the meat and mix it well with the bread crumbs, half the milk, the onion, half the salt, the hot pepper sauce, marjoram, and tarragon. Shape it into 1 in. balls and drop into the water that by now should be boiling. Let simmer for 10 minutes.

In a large saucepan cook your noodles as per package instructions while—wipe your brow—in a small saucepan you make the sauce by combining the flour with the sour cream and the remaining salt. Over low heat, and stirring constantly, add the remaining 1/2 cup milk to this, together with paprika, and continue stirring until smooth and thick. By now the meatballs have simmered long enough. Drain them into a colander and return to their pan, pouring the cream sauce over. Over very, very low heat so that the sauce doesn't boil, heat everything through. Drain your noodles into colander, return to their pot, and toss with butter or margarine and poppy seed. Serve with glasses of beer, and for salad use packaged cole slaw tossed with a bottled oil-and-vinegar dressing.

We all know that little girls are made of "sugar and spice, and all that's nice," and we wouldn't be without any of the ingredients, right? The same holds true for the next recipe, so if you don't have some of the spices mentioned, do me a favor and pick them up from your grocer's spice shelf.

MEDITERRANEAN MEATBALLS
(4 Servings)

1 med. onion, minced *or*
1-2 tsp. instant minced onion
1 med. green pepper, minced
1/4 tsp. garlic powder
2 tsp. ground coriander
2 tsp. salt
1/2 tsp. cinnamon
1/4 tsp. ground cloves
1/4 tsp. ground cardamon
1/2 tsp. chili powder
1/2 tsp. hot pepper sauce
1 egg, beaten
1 lb. ground beef
4 tbsp. butter or margarine
1 10-oz. can beef consommé
1 small can evaporated milk
1 pkg. beef-flavored rice

While the rice is cooking as per package instructions, mix all other ingredients except butter or margarine, consommé, and evaporated milk. Make sure all spices are really worked into the meat before you melt the butter or margarine and shape the meat mixture into 12 balls. Brown well on all sides in melted butter before adding consommé and evaporated milk to skillet; reduce heat, cover, and let simmer for about 15 minutes. Serve with the rice, and to stay with the Mediterranean theme have sliced cucumbers tossed in a yogurt-and-lemon dressing for salad.

Since this is a rather spicy dish that might remind some palates more used to bland food of the quote from the Bible, "Can a man take fire in his bosom, and his clothes not be burned?" you may want to follow it with this dessert . . . soothing in spite of its fiery name.

FLAMING BANANAS
(4 Servings)

3 tbsp. butter or margarine
3/4 cup firmly packed brown sugar
1/4 cup dark rum
3 bananas, peeled and sliced
1 pint vanilla ice cream
2 tbsp. dark rum

With all the ingredients at hand, this can be fixed at the table or you may repair to the kitchen where in a medium-sized skillet you melt the butter or margarine before adding the brown sugar, stirring until throughly blended. Pour in 1/4 cup of the rum before you peel and slice the bananas into it. Let it simmer for about 5 minutes, turn off heat, pour remaining rum over, ignite, stir until flames die down, then serve over scoops of ice cream.

Even if you don't keep hard-boiled eggs on standby in the refrigerator, which really is a great help at odd times, this dish can still come in under the thirty-minute wire. While the eggs are boiling you can prepare everything else and still find that John Wesley was right when he said, "Though I am always in haste, I am never in a hurry."

Incidentally, do you know how to tell a hard-boiled egg from a raw one when they're both in the shell? Very easy . . . just spin them. The hard-boiled one will spin with grace and speed whereas the raw one sort of wobbles.

MEXICAN MEATBALLS
(3-4 Servings)

1/2 lb. ground beef
1/2 lb. ground pork
6 eggs, hard-boiled
2 green onions, finely diced
1/2 tsp. crumbled bay leaves
1/4 tsp. dried mint
1/2 tsp. marjoram
1 tsp. salt
1/4 tsp. white pepper
2-3 tbsp. butter or margarine
1/4 cup milk
1/4 cup water
1-2 tsp. Worcestershire sauce
1 1-lb. can potatoes, drained
1 tbsp. butter or margarine
Parsley

Peel the hard-boiled eggs, cut in halves, put yolks aside and chop the whites. Mix together the ground meats with the chopped whites, the diced green onion, bay leaves, mint, marjoram, salt, and pepper. While you melt the butter or margarine in a deep skillet shape the meat mixture into 12 balls around the 12 yolk halves. Now brown them well on all sides, reduce heat, and let simmer for about 10 to 15 minutes, while you sauté the drained potatoes in remaining butter or margarine for about 5 minutes before tossing them with parsley. At that time also add milk, water, and Worcestershire sauce to skillet drippings and let heat through before you serve the food with foamy glasses of beer.

You're rushed for time more than usual . . . can't even make that trip to the market . . . and you still have to get dinner on the table. Maybe the next recipe will solve your problem since you are apt to have most of the ingredients on hand . . . if not, the nearest liquor-deli will. In either case you can fix this quickly and when you serve it you may quote A. A. Milne's Winnie the Pooh line: "Time for a little something." As any Pooh fan knows this means something good.

RICEY MEATBALLS
(3-4 Servings)

1 lb. ground beef
2 tsp. instant minced onion
2 tbsp. fine bread crumbs
1/2 tsp. salt
1/4 tsp. nutmeg
1 egg, beaten
1-2 tbsp. butter or margarine
1 10-oz. can cream of mushroom soup
1/2 cup dry sherry
1/2 cup water
1/2 tsp. dill weed
1/4 tsp. marjoram
1 beef bouillon cube
1 10-oz. pkg. frozen peas
1 1/3 cup quick-cooking rice

In a bowl mix together well the meat with the onion, breadcrumbs, salt, and nutmeg, binding it with the beaten egg. While you melt the butter or margarine in a deep skillet, shape the meat mixture into 12 balls. Brown meatballs well on all sides before adding mushroom soup, sherry, water, beef bouillon cube, dill, marjoram, and peas to skillet. Bring to boil, stir in quick-cooking rice, reduce heat, and let simmer for 10 to 15 minutes—or until most of the liquid is absorbed.

Serve a crisp green salad and for dessert have canned peach halves, filled with ice cream and drenched with chocolate fudge sauce. Or, if you are calorie-conscious, sherbet.

Nothing says German cooking better than sauerbraten, and this next recipe will bring back all your fondest memories of this dish . . . without all the time and effort needed to produce it. However, since it's marginal to bring it in within the allotted thirty minutes, I have included the recipe for an easy chicken soup, which you can savour while the meatballs finish simmering. After all, who wants to be called a liar over 5 minutes?

SAUERBRATEN MEATBALLS
(3-4 Servings)

1 lb. ground beef
1/4 cup dry bread crumbs
1/3 cup minced onion *or,*
1 tsp. instant minced onion
1 tsp. salt
1/4 tsp. caraway seed
2/3 cup evaporated milk
2 tbsp. butter or margarine
1 10-oz. can beer
2 tbsp. vinegar
2 tbsp. ketchup
1 tbsp. brown sugar
8 whole peppercorns
1/2 tsp. crumbled bay leaves
1/3 cup raisins
6 gingersnaps, crushed
2 1-lb. can potatoes, drained
2 tbsp. butter or margarine
Parsley

106 The Thirty Minute Dinner

In a mixing bowl blend together well the beef, bread crumbs, onion, salt, caraway seed, and milk. While you shape it into 12 meatballs melt the butter or margarine in a large skillet and over medium heat brown the balls well on all sides. Keep an eye on them while you fix the sauce in a small bowl by combining beer, vinegar, ketchup brown sugar, peppercorns, bay leaves, raisins, and crushed gingersnaps. This last is easily done in a small plastic bag with a rolling pin or empty bottle, and that way you avoid having to wash the blender. Pour sauce over browned meatballs, stir gently to assure everything is well covered and coated and simmer for about 20 to 25 minutes under cover, stirring it once in a while ever so gently. About 5 minutes before you're ready to serve, melt the remaining butter or margarine in a small saucepan and sauté the drained potatoes in this, under cover, before tossing them with parsley. Serve meatballs right out of skillet, adjusting for salt if you go heavy on that, and have beer and pickles ready for those who might like them.

Now for the chicken soup you fix right after you start your potatoes:

HERBED CHICKEN SOUP
(3-4 Servings)

2 10-oz. cans clear chicken broth
1 soup can water
1/2 cup dry white wine

1 tbsp. parsley flakes
1/4 tsp. thyme
1 tbsp. green onion tops, snipped
1/4 tsp. rosemary
Cheese croutons

Bring chicken broth, wine, and water to a slow boil together with the herbs and let simmer for about 3 minutes before serving in dainty soup bowls, strained. If you don't have a strainer, simply run a paper towel across the top and most of the herbs will adhere to that. Sprinkle cheese croutons on top and you're all set.

In spite of geographically originating from the same spot this next recipe is quite different from the Mexican Meatballs, but equally good and a great hit with kids of all ages. As John Dryden put it: "Men are but children of a larger growth."

SOUTH-OF-THE-BORDER MEATBALLS
(4 Servings)

1 lb. ground beef
1/4 cup yellow corn meal
2 tsp. instant minced onion
1-2 tsp. salt
1/2 tsp. black pepper
1 tsp. chili powder
2/3 cup evaporated milk (small can)
2 tbsp. flour
1/4 cup butter or margarine
2 1 lb. cans tomatoes
1 1-lb. can whole kernel corn, drained
1/2 tsp. sweet basil
1/2 tsp. thyme

In a bowl, with your hands, mix the ground beef well with the corn meal, onion, 1 tsp. salt, pepper, chili powder, and evaporated milk. Shape into 12 meatballs and, while the butter or margarine is melting in a deep skillet, roll the meatballs in flour. Brown well on all sides before adding all other ingredients to the skillet. Bring to a boil, reduce heat, and let simmer for 15 to 20 minutes under cover.

Serve with tortillas you have buttered and heated in the oven in a stack (you can get them in the freezer department of the grocer's deli) and beer.

Since chocolate is inherent to much of Mexican cooking, why not have chocolate ice cream with toasted shredded coconut for dessert. You've already turned on the oven, right?

NOTES

The Thirty Minute Dinner

I must admit that whenever I see a marquee or billboard boldly stating, "Repeated by popular request," I have always assumed it was a cop-out on the part of the management, or that the popular request was their own echo. But in repeating this next recipe, originally appearing in my *One Pot Dinner*, I'm giving in to the many requests for it from viewers who saw it demonstrated on television. Since it qualifies both as a one-pot dinner and as a thirty-minute dinner, I once more send thanks to my Javanese friend in Copenhagen.

KIMA
(3-4 Servings)

1 med. onion, finely chopped
2 tbsp. butter or margarine
1/2 tsp. salt
1/2 tsp. ground cumin
1/2 tsp. turmeric
1/2 tsp. ginger
1 dash black pepper
1 dash garlic powder
1 dash cayenne
1/2 tsp. crumbled bay leaves
2 large potatoes, pared and diced
1 lb. ground beef
1 10-oz. pkg. frozen peas
1 large tomato, chopped
1 tsp. meat sauce, (BV, Bovril, etc.)
1/4 cup hot water

In a heavy saucepan with a tight-fitting cover, melt the butter or margarine while you chop the onion and saute in this for about 5 minutes, under cover, until translucent and limp. Add salt, cumin, turmeric, ginger, pepper, garlic powder, cayenne, and bay leaves—it's easier if you've mixed them all first in an egg cup or small glass—stir, and sauté for about 1 to 2 minutes before you add the cubed potatoes you prepared while the onion was sautéeing. Cook for about 5 minutes, making sure the potatoes don't scorch. Now add the ground meat, broken up, and brown evenly throughout. Add the peas, tomato, and meat sauce. Stir and cover tightly. Reduce heat and let simmer for about 15 to 20 minutes or until potatoes are done. Add a little water if the dish gets too dry . . . the finished product should be just moist, not stewy-juicy.

Have hard-crust dinner rolls on hand as well as some beer, which goes nicely with this. A piece of cheesecake makes a good dessert.

The Thirty Minute Dinner

According to Robert Louis Stevenson, "Man is a creature who lives not on bread alone, but principally by catchwords." Be that as it may be, it would seem to me that Mr. Stevenson for once painted himself into a corner, it is certain that he could never have met a Swedish man . . . they live by Beef Lindstrom. This dish is not nearly as well-known as it deserves, so let me introduce you to this delightful Swedish staff of life.

BEEF LINDSTROM
(4 Servings)

1 egg, beaten
1/2 tsp. hot pepper sauce
2 tsp. salt
3/4 cup milk
2 tsp. instant minced onion
1 lb. ground beef
1 1-lb. can potatoes, drained and diced *or* the equivalent in cooked potatoes
3/4 cup pickled beets, diced
2 tbsp. juice from beets
6 tbsp. butter or margarine
6 eggs
2 tbsp. capers—*optional*

Get two large skillets out—one for the meat patties, one big enough to fry six eggs in. Now in a medium-sized bowl beat 1 egg, stir in pepper sauce, salt, milk, and instant onion. Mix in the broken-up ground beef. When well

Beef 113

blended add the diced potatoes, beets, and beet juice, stirring until throughly mixed. While you shape the mixture into six patties melt 4 tbsp. butter or margarine in one skillet, and fry the meat patties well on both sides until done . . . you know best how pink or well-done you like them. When I do it I let them simmer for 5 minutes after they're brown. In the other skillet melt the remaining butter or margarine, break your six eggs into this, and fry. Place fried eggs on top of meat patties, garnish with capers, and carry proudly to the table where you should have some good rye bread, sweet butter, and glasses of beer waiting, together with your favorite pickles.

For dessert have fruit and cheese . . . but if you really want to please somebody for whom Sweden is a personal paradise . . . go to the trouble of having first fixed the Applesauce-Almond Bake on Page 75, because in the words of Emerson, "A friend may well be reckoned the masterpiece of nature"; . . . which brings me to this next recipe.

You may all have enjoyed the film *Alice's Restaurant* or the food from her cook book, but I believe I am the only one who can boast an original "Alice's Kitchen." After thumbing through the sketchbook of a teenage, talented friend, Alice by name, I let her loose in my kitchen . . . and the result is one of the happiest things you can imagine. With each drawer painted in different shades of red, yellow, and green, and happy "op" drawings on all the cupboards, even the worst chore in the kitchen becomes a fun thing that makes you whistle and scurry along. I highly recommend the therapeutic values of such surroundings.

But my friend's sunshine personality is not limited to her art work. Throughly interested in food, she shines at cooking as well, as represented by the following main-course salad . . . good any day for dinner, but on a hot summer evening you may want to accompany it with the buttermilk cooler I have included—a Danish calorie-conscious version of the popular American milk shake.

ALICE'S MEATY SUNSHINE SALAD
(4-6 Servings)

3/4 lb. breakfast steaks
2 tbsp. butter or margarine
1/2 head of lettuce, shredded fine
1 bunch watercress, chopped
1 bunch green onions, diced fine
1 green pepper, seeded and
   diced fine
6-8 mushrooms, washed and sliced
2 5-oz. cans boned chicken, drained
1 cucumber, diced
12 cherry tomatoes, washed and
   cut in halves
1 8-oz. can whole kernel corn, drained

Dressing:

Drippings from breakfast steak
1/3 cup vinegar, preferably red wine
1/4 cup olive oil
1 - 2 tsp. seasoned salt

1/2 tsp. lemon pepper *or* **regular pepper**
2 tbsp. **imitation bacon bits**
1 - 2 tsp. **Worcestershire sauce**
1/4 tsp. **dry mustard**

    Melt the butter in a medium-sized skillet while you cut the breakfast steaks into 1/4 in. strips and brown them well in this while you start fixing the greens. Turn heat off meat and let cool in drippings. Shred your lettuce fine and get out a big salad bowl that will hold everything. Put lettuce into bowl, followed by watercress—which you have chopped after cutting off stems—the finely diced green onions, the green pepper in likewise condition, the raw sliced mushrooms, and the diced cucumber, peeled or unpeeled as you prefer. Tear your canned chicken into shreds and put into bowl, together with the meat strips you have lifted out of the skillet with a slotted spoon.
    Then pour the drained corn over all and sprinkle the tomato halves on top.
    Now for the dressing . . . into a large measuring cup pour the drippings from the skillet and add all remaining ingredients, blend well, and pour over salad. Toss gently and with love, and serve with hard-crust rolls, either accompanied or followed by the Buttermilk Cooler.

The Thirty Minute Dinner

Even if you're not too fond of buttermilk, do try this next recipe. It may not change your life, but I am pretty sure it will change your attitude toward buttermilk.

BUTTERMILK COOLER
(6-8 Servings)

3 eggs
1/2 cup sugar
2 tbsp. grated lemon peel
2 qt. chilled buttermilk
1/2 tsp. vanilla extract

Break the eggs into a large bowl and beat until thick and foamy. Gradually add the sugar, beating well after each addition, stir in the lemon peel — the kind you get in a jar from the grocer's spice shelf or the fresh kind if you have a lemon handy—the chilled buttermilk, and the vanilla extract, stirring until well blended. If you have a blender, you can, of course, do everything in that.

CHICKEN

Robert Louis Stevenson once stated, "Politics is perhaps the only profession for which no preparation is necessary,..." a comment I am not about to touch with a ten foot pole, except as further proof that I would not fit into politics, because I do like to prepare.

Holding in high regard such advice as Cervantes' "To be prepared is half the victory," and such proverbs as "Have not thy cloak to make when it begins to rain"; "A stitch in time saves nine"; and "A man surprised is half beaten"; I am the type who tapes lists of what I'm packing inside my suitcases so I won't forget anything when I pack at the other end, and sits down for an hour once a week trying to plan the week's activities, including what to serve for dinner when. The fact that I still need a memory course to sometimes remember where I put all the lists is inconsequential . . . I know I'll be prepared when I find them.

I don't go quite as far as my grandmother did—she not only kept track of what to serve in the future, she also had a file of whom she'd entertained for dinner, what she had served, and what she'd worn with whom . . . all of which are things I sometimes wish I had done.

An idea I did pick up from her is what she called her "unexpected corner" in the pantry, a corner that made it possible for her at the drop of my grandfather's hat to serve unexpected guests with more than a cracker. The mainstay of her "corner" was cold chicken, boiled and roasted, and to this day you can open my refrigerator door and find one of each tucked away in a corner, prepared when I was otherwise occupied in the kitchen . . . and lifesavers on numerous occasions . . . not to mention the money saved by not having to call out to a commercial house when suddenly faced with late unexpected guests.

So to get the full advantage in the most economical way of the next chapter, may I humbly suggest that you follow in my grandmother's footsteps and keep a cold bird in your larder for your man. That way you can quickly turn it into a hot bird and live up to Eugene Field's words:

> *When I demanded of my friend what viands*
> *he preferred,*
> *He quoth: "A large cold bottle, and a small*
> *hot bird!"*

However, since we live in an age of convenience you may, of course, substitute canned chicken wherever it says "cooked"; but being a nut for homemade things, always subconsciously humming the lines from Gilbert and Sullivan's *H.M.S. Pinafore:*

> *Things are seldom what they seem,*
> *Skim milk masquerades as cream;*

I'll stick with my bird in the refrigerator.

CHICKEN BAKE
(4 Servings)

2 cups cooked or canned chicken
1 4-oz. can water chestnuts, sliced
4 stalks celery, diced
1 green pepper, seeded and diced
1 bunch green onions, sliced
3/4 cup mayonnaise
1/2 - 1 tsp. seasoned salt
1/4 tsp. white pepper
1/2 tsp. sweet basil
1 - 2 tsp. curry—*optional*
1 tbsp. lemon juice, bottled
1 large tomato, sliced
3/4 cup grated Parmesan cheese
1/4 cup dry bread crumbs
1 - 2 tbsp. butter or margarine

Set the oven at 350° and grease a 2-qt. baking dish. Mix the chicken meat that you have torn into bite-size pieces with the drained, sliced water chestnuts, diced celery, and pepper, plus the sliced green onions. In a small bowl mix mayonnaise with salt, pepper, basil, curry—if you want to use it—and lemon juice, and toss the chicken mixture with this. Top with the sliced tomato, and sprinkle bread crumbs and cheese on top of that before dotting with a little extra butter. Since we all want to save on the dishes, you should have done all this in the greased baking dish. Cover and bake for 20 to 25 minutes, serving it with hard-crust dinner rolls you've heated along for the last 10 minutes.

For dessert you can have fresh fruit, but since you've got the oven going anyway, you might want to take advantage of that and try this dessert which you can fix and start baking while the chicken is in the oven.

BAKED MINCEMEAT PEACHES
(4 Servings)

> 4 - 6 large, canned peach halves
> 1 cup prepared mincemeat
> 2 tbsp. dry sherry
> 1/4 cup granulated sugar
> 1 tbsp. cornstarch
> 1 pinch of salt
> 2/3 cup syrup from peaches
> 1 tsp. grated lemon peel
> 1 tbsp. lemon juice, bottled
> 1 tbsp. butter or margarine

Lightly butter a small, pretty baking dish and place 4 to 6 drained, canned peach halves in it (the largest ones possible), reserving the syrup. Mix mincemeat with sherry and divide among the peaches. Bake in your preheated oven for about 15 to 20 minutes, at around 350° to 375°. Serve warm with lemon sauce made by heating the peach syrup in a small saucepan into which you have carefully sifted and mixed the cornstarch, sugar, and pinch of salt, cooking until clear and thickened, about 5 minutes. Remove saucepan from heat, blend in the lemon peel, lemon juice, and butter, stir, and serve warm over the warm peaches.

NOTES

The next four recipes all call for chicken breasts—boned—but don't let that scare you. Most butchers will do this for you for a slight charge; but should you run into an unfriendly one, you still don't have to despair. Done with a sharp, pointed knife when the meat is still semi-frozen from the meat tray, it becomes a breeze. The first recipe keeps you pretty busy most of the time so don't plan on getting involved in any conversation...just concentrate on the work at hand.

CHINESE CHICKEN
(4 Servings)

4 chicken breasts, skinned and boned
1/2 lb. lean pork, in strips
2 tbsp. vegetable oil
1 - 2 tsp. salt
1 - 2 tsp. ground ginger
1 tbsp. soy sauce
1 8-oz. can bamboo shoots, drained
1 4-oz. can mushroom pieces, drained
1 9-oz. pkg. frozen broccoli, partially defrosted
1 inner heart of celery, diced, tops and all
1 med. onion, chopped
1 10-oz. can chicken broth
2 tbsp. cornstarch
1 tsp. sugar
1/2 cup water
1 8-oz. can pineapple chunks, drained
1 8-oz. can peas, drained
1/2 cup blanched almonds, toasted
Chinese noodles

While you cut the boned chicken and lean pork in strips, heat the oil in a large, deep, skillet, sprinkle oil with salt, and lightly brown your meats in this while you chop the onion and dice the celery. Sprinkle ginger and soy sauce over meat mixture, and stir well, before adding drained bamboo shoots, mushrooms, broccoli, celery, and onion. Give it all a good stir and let simmer for about 5 minutes. Pour the chicken broth in and continue simmering for another 5 minutes. Mix cornstarch and sugar with water, stir in, and cook until thickened, a couple of minutes. Now add your peas and pineapple chunks, adjust for salt and continue cooking for 3 to 5 minutes, until everything is heated through, while you lightly toast the blanched almonds in a 350° oven. Sprinkle these on top and serve with Chinese noodles on the side.

For a beverage you can have beer, sake, or for that matter, tea...and some anise or almond cookies make a nice dessert.

This next recipe is more delicate in flavor and texture and deserves to be presented on your best china. As Andrew Lang wrote:

> *There's a joy without canker or cark,*
> *There's a pleasure eternally new,*
> *'Tis to gloat on the glaze and mark*
> *Of china that's ancient and blue.*

And if you don't believe Mr. Lang, just think what it has done for those ladies in the TV detergent commercials.

CHICKEN WITH CHINESE MUSHROOMS
(3 Servings)

3 chicken breasts, skinned and boned
6 dried Chinese mushrooms
1 med. onion, chopped
1 green pepper, thinly sliced
1/2 celery heart, in 1/2 in. pieces
4 tbsp. peanut oil *or* any vegetable oil
1/2 tsp. ground ginger
1/2 cup water
1/2 cup dry sherry
2 chicken bouillon cubes
1 - 2 tbsp. cornstarch
2 tbsp. soy sauce
Chinese noodles

Cover the dried Chinese mushrooms you've bought in a Chinese grocery store with warm water and let soak for 10 munutes. Now chop the onion, and slice the green pepper and celery. Add half the oil to a large skillet, heat well and sauté the three vegetables, under cover, for about 5 minutes, while you slice the boned chicken meat—remember the friendly butcher. By now it should be time to drain the mushrooms. Snip off the tough stems and cut mushrooms into halves or quarters into a small saucepan. Sprinkle mushrooms with ginger, add bouillon cubes, and pour water and sherry over; bring to a boil and let simmer for 10 minutes. Remove vegetable mixture temporarily from large skillet with a slotted spoon, heat remaining oil well and sauté chicken strips. When chicken is lightly browned, return vegetable to skillet, pour mushrooms and stock over, and continue simmering. Now mix your cornstarch with the soy sauce, add to skillet, and continue cooking for another 2 to 3 minutes. Serve with Chinese noodles on the side . . . and either have almond cookies or cheesecake for dessert.

The next two recipes are delicate—almost dainty—but don't let that keep you from serving them to the man in your life . . . he'll appreciate their subtle flavors. Both recipes are enhanced by a chilled glass of wine, proving once more the truth of John Gay's little poem:

> *Fill ev'ry glass, for wine inspires us,*
>   *And fires us*
> *With courage, love and joy.*

CREAMED LEMONY CHICKEN BREASTS
(3-4 Servings)

3 chicken breasts, split, skinned, and boned
1 tsp. salt
1/2 tsp. pepper
1/4 tsp. rosemary, crushed
8 tbsp. butter or margarine (1 cube)
8 green onions, diced
1/4 cup dry sherry
2 tsp. lemon peel, dried
2 tbsp. bottled lemon juice
1 cup cream
2 tbsp. butter or margarine
1 1-lb. can potatoes, drained
1 1-lb. can green beans, drained
1 - 2 tbsp. butter or margarine
1 tsp. dill weed
1/4 cup grated Parmesan cheese

While you dice the green onions, melt 2 tbsp. of the butter or margarine in an ovenproof dish on top of the stove. Sprinkle crushed rosemary into butter, stir in green onions, and let sauté, under cover, for 5 minutes. If you didn't have the butcher bone the chicken breasts for you, do this now with a sharp knife, winding up with six halves. Sprinkle meat with salt and pepper, lift the sautéed onion out of the dish to a warm platter, add the remaining butter or margarine, turn heat up a little, and brown the six chicken breasts well on both sides—this takes about 5 to 7 minutes. Pour in sherry, lemon juice, the bottled kind, and lemon peel, the kind you found on the grocer's spice shelf, and let this cook for about 2 minutes before you return the onions to the dish, slowly also adding the cream. Turn heat down to low and let simmer, under cover, while you heat the drained, canned potatoes in a little butter in one saucepan, and sauté the drained canned beans in another in 2 tbsp. butter or margarine to which you have added the dill weed. Toss beans well before serving—and for once will I deviate from my rule of serving right out of the pot. Put your two vegetables in a double dish, if you have one, or two pretty china dishes, and serve chicken right out of baking dish after you've sprinkled it with Parmesan cheese and run it under the broiler for a minute or two.

Serve with a dry, chilled white wine and croissant dinner rolls. If strawberries are in season, for dessert try and serve a box of washed and hulled strawberries you have sprinkled with sugar and tossed in 2/3 cup of dry white wine.

DAINTY CHICKEN BREASTS
(2-3 Servings)

2 chicken breasts, boned, skinned, and cut in halves
1/4 cup dry fine bread crumbs
1 egg, beaten
1 tsp. salt
2 tbsp. butter or margarine
1 cup pineapple juice
2 tbsp. lemon juice
1 tbsp. cornstarch
1/2 tsp. curry powder
1 tbsp. sugar
1 pkg. curried rice
Blanched, slivered almonds

Split and bone the chicken breasts, unless you had your friendly butcher take care of that. While you melt the butter or margarine in a deep, large skillet, dip the pieces of chicken first in the well-beaten egg, then the bread crumbs. Sprinkle with salt and brown on both sides, while you start cooking the curried rice according to package instructions. When the chicken is browned, pour off excess fat and add the pineapple juice you've mixed with cornstarch, curry, and sugar. Cover skillet and let simmer for 20 minutes, at which time both rice and chicken should be done. Sprinkle the slivered almonds on top of chicken and serve, with a salad of avocado and tomato slices, tossed in a lemon juice and oil dressing.

Have a bottle of wine chilled in the refrigerator and for dessert have assorted little pastries from your favorite continental bake shop.

For this next recipe you will need two skillets, a pot, and an ovenproof dish, an array that sounds as if it may lead to a lot of confusion, but it really doesn't . . . and you even have time to get rid of the used pots and pans before you serve dinner.

CHICK-A' LEEK BAKE
(4 Servings)

1 1/2 cups cooked or canned chicken
1/2 of 1 8-oz. pkg. noodles
4 tbsp. butter or margarine
3 large leeks, washed and sliced
1 large green pepper, cut in strips
1 tsp. salt
1/2 tsp. rosemary, crushed
2 - 3 tbsp. flour
1 cup milk
1/2 cup water
1/2 cup dry white wine
2 chicken bouillon cubes
6 slices bacon

Set oven at 350°. In a medium-sized pot cook noodles according to package instructions. Get out two skillets; melt the butter or margarine in one while you slice the leeks (discard the reedy part of the greens) and green pepper; sprinkle salt and rosemary into butter, add vegetables, stir, and let sauté, under cover, for about 7 minutes. In the other skillet fry the bacon to a crisp and drain on a paper towel. When the vegetables are done, sprinkle with flour and then gradually add the milk, water, wine, and bouillon cubes. Bring to a slight bubble, making sure it doesn't get lumpy—a wire whisk is good for that —before you add the chicken meat, torn or cut into bite-size pieces. By now your noodles should be done. Drain them into a colander, grease a 2-qt. baking dish, mix noodles and skillet mixture well in baking dish before you crumble the bacon on top and bake for 15 minutes.

Serve with sliced tomatoes, coated in oil and vinegar, and hard-crust dinner rolls. Fresh fruit is all you need for dessert.

This next dish is one of my favorites and goes over very well with men.

CURRIED CHICKEN BROCCOLI BAKE
(3-4 Servngs)

2 cups cooked or canned chicken
   in fairly large pieces
2 10-oz. pkgs. of frozen broccoli
1 10-oz. can of cream of mushroom soup
2/3 cup mayonnaise
1/3 cup evaporated milk
1/2 cup grated Cheddar cheese
1 tsp. bottled lemon juice
1 - 2 tsp. curry powder
8 large mushrooms, washed and sliced
1/2 cup fine dry bread crumbs
1 - 2 tbsp. butter or margarine

Set oven at 350°. While you partially cook the frozen broccoli according to package instructions, lavishly grease a 2-qt. baking dish and blend, in a medium-sized bowl, the cream of mushroom soup with the mayonnaise, evaporated milk, grated cheese, lemon juice, and curry. Drain broccoli in colander, wash and slice the mushrooms, and with kitchen tongs place the warm broccoli in bottom of baking dish. On top of this arrange first the chicken pieces, then the sliced mushrooms, and cover all with your mayonnaise-cheese mixture. Sprinkle with bread crumbs, dot with butter or margarine and bake for 20 to 25 minutes for an absolutely scrumptious dish. I don't use salt in this dish, but you may want to, so taste the mayonnaise mixture and add it there if you feel it needs it.

Serve with hard-crust dinner rolls. And sliced tomatoes in an oil-and vinegar dressing not only taste good with this, they also add a nice color touch. For dessert all you need is coffee and some good candy.

NOTES

If you are one of those people who like to cook right at the table under the admiring and hopefully approving eyes of your hungry guests, this next recipe lends itself very well to that, but until you get the hang of it you may prefer the privacy of your kitchen. There is nothing wrong with living up to John Gay's plea:

> *Give me, kind heaven, a private station*
> *A mind serene for contemplation!*

while you prepare for your guests or family's pleasure. On the contrary . . . as Moliere said: "It is a wonderful seasoning of all enjoyments to think of those we love."

MONGOLIAN CHICKEN
(2-3 Servings)

2 whole chicken breasts, boned
2 tablespoons butter
6 green onions, diced, tops and all
1 large green pepper, seeded and cut in strips
6 large mushrooms, washed and sliced
1/2 tsp. oregano
1/2 tsp. marjoram
1/4 tsp. garlic powder
1 tsp. salt
1/4 tsp. pepper
1/4 cup lemon juice
1/4 cup soy sauce
1/4 cup dry white wine
1 4-oz. can shoestring potatoes

Clean and prepare the vegetables and sauté in skillet in melted butter, adding the herbs and garlic powder. Sauté for about 5 minutes after you've stirred it well to make sure everything is coated. If you didn't have your butcher bone the chicken for you, do this now, and cut it into bite-size pieces. Don't worry—there's enough time for it. Now push the vegetables to one side of skillet, add more butter or margarine if necessary, and quickly brown the chicken slices or pieces. Stir all together, sprinkle with salt and pepper, pour the lemon juice which you have mixed with wine and soy sauce over all, give it one more stir and let simmer, under cover, for about 5 to 7 minutes. Serve with shoestring potatoes on the side and remember your guests might be like Diogenes who when asked what wine he liked to drink, replied: "That which belongs to another"; so have a bottle of chilled, white wine in the refrigerator ready for such an emergency.

For dessert serve whatever fresh fruit is in season—if it happens to be strawberries, why not try these:

DREAMY STRAWBERRIES
(2-3 Servings)

1 box fresh strawberries, washed and hulled
4 tsp. sugar
3 tbsp. orange juice
3 tbsp. **Curaco** *or* **Triple Sec**
1/2 cup heavy cream, whipped

Sprinkle sugar over the cleaned strawberries, pour orange juice and liqueur over, whip the cream very stiff, and gently toss strawberries in this. Chill until ready to serve.

NOTES

These next two recipes take their inspiration from the Italian risotto and the Greek pilaf, but the transference to American cooking was successful, and since they keep you in the kitchen for no more than ten minutes they might turn into some of your more trusted standbys on busy days.

RICEY CHICKEN AMANDINE
(4 Servings)

2 10-oz. cans chicken broth
2 tsp. instant minced onion
2 tbsp. butter or margarine
1 cup half-and-half
1 2-oz. can pimiento, diced
1 cup raw rice
2 1/2 cups cooked, diced chicken
1/4 tsp. nutmeg
1/2 tsp. thyme
1/4 tsp. marjoram
1 tsp. salt
1/2 cup blanched, toasted almonds

In a medium-sized saucepan bring the chicken broth, instant onion, and butter or margarine to a boil; add the half-and-half and just before it boils again add all the other ingredients, with the exception of the almonds. Lower flame and simmer, under cover, for 15 minutes. Take a peak, give it a stir and continue simmering for another 10 minutes, while in a low oven or a small skillet you toast the almonds. Sprinkle toasted almonds on top and serve with a good, crisp salad on the side.

For dessert all you need is your favorite cookies and coffee.

RICEY CHICKEN ORANGE
(4 Servings)

2 cups cooked chicken, in bite-size pieces
1 small onion, chopped
1 small green pepper, chopped
2 - 3 tbsp. butter or margarine
1/2 tsp. dried mint
1/4 tsp. dry mustard
1 1/2 cups orange juice
1 cup dry white wine
2 chicken bouillon cubes
1 tsp. salt
1/4 tsp. white pepper
1 cup raw rice

While the butter or margarine is melting in a medium-sized saucepan, chop the onion and wash and chop the green pepper. Sauté them, under cover, in the butter for about 5 minutes, sprinkled with mustard and dried mint. Pour the orange juice and white wine over, add the bouillon cubes, salt, and pepper, bring to a boil and add raw rice and chicken. Lower the heat, cover, and let simmer for 15 minutes. Check for salt, give it a good stir, continue simmering for another 10 minutes, and you're ready to serve this colorful dish.

Sliced marinated tomatoes make a good salad for it, and for dessert, a cheese tray is all that's needed.

NOTES

This next recipe for cold chicken salad is just different enough from the more standard versions to make it a conversation piece, illustrating very well Oscar Wilde's statement: "There is only one thing in the world worse than being talked about, and that is not being talked about." —a thought most people subconsciously agree with, but very rarely admit to.

Anyway, the salad deserves to be talked about and can also double as a luncheon dish. Should you be worried it isn't quite substantial enough for the more hearty appetites, I have included in the menu an easy-to-fix and tasty hot soup.

CHICKEN-VEGETABLE SALAD
(4 Servings)

2 cups cooked or canned chicken, in bite-size pieces
8 large mushrooms, washed and sliced
1 large green pepper, seeded and chopped
1 1-lb. can whole kernel corn, drained
1 8-oz. can peas, drained
1 cup mayonnaise
1/2 tsp. dill weed
1/4 tsp. nutmeg
1/2 tsp. salt or to taste
3 hard-boiled eggs

If you don't have hard-boiled eggs in the refrigerator, start by boiling them for about 12 minutes, before you shell them under running, cold water. While they're boiling, wash and slice your mushrooms and dice the green pepper. In the bowl you plan to serve the salad in, mix the chicken meat with the mushrooms, green pepper, drained corn, and peas. In a small bowl blend together the mayonnaise, salt, dill weed, and nutmeg; fold this into chicken mixture, making sure everything is coated. Top with the hard-boiled eggs, cut in halves, and serve with hard-crust dinner rolls.

Since you certainly have time to fix something else should you want to make a more hearty meal out of dinner, try this:

PEA SOUP SUPREME
(4 Servings)

1 small onion, chopped
1 stalk celery, diced
1-2 tbsp. butter or margarine
1/2 tsp. sweet basil
1/2 tsp. dried mint
2 10-oz. cans pea soup
1 1/2 cups water
1/2 cup dry white wine
1 cup canned tomatoes, chopped
Croutons

In a saucepan melt the butter or margarine while you chop the onion and dice the celery; sauté vegetables in this, under cover, for about 5 minutes, sprinkled with the sweet basil and dried mint. Stir in the pea soup, gradually add water and wine, together with the chopped tomatoes, and cook over low heat until heated through and lightly bubbly. Serve with your favorite croutons sprinkled on top—cheese croutons add a nice touch.

NOTES

The Thirty Minute Dinner

I may be taking a genetic liberty by including this next recipe for squab under chicken . . . but surely they're closely related. The dish is the kind you would want to fix for your fellow on a very special occasion—the kind that brings to mind these sage words by Oscar Wilde: "Men always want to be a woman's first love. That is their clumsy vanity. Women have a more subtle instinct about things. They want to be man's last romance."

SHERRIED SQUAB
(2 Servings)

2 squabs, thawed
4 large mushrooms, washed
   and finely chopped
1 - 2 tbsp. butter or margarine
1/4 cup fine, dry bread crumbs
1/2 cup pecans, chopped fine
1/4 tsp. salt
1/8 tsp. black pepper
1/2 cup dry sherry
Milk
2 slices bacon, cut in halves
1/2 pkg. wild rice
1 10-oz. pkg. frozen asparagus

Set oven at 475°. While the butter or margarine is melting in a small skillet, wash and finely chop the mushrooms before sautéing them in it, under cover, for about 4-5 minutes. Add the dry bread crumbs and pecans, together with salt and pepper. Stir in 1 tbsp. of the sherry and just enough milk to bind it all together. Remove from heat and stuff the cavities of the two birds with this. Grease a shallow baking pan and put the squabs in this, breast side up. Put the slices of bacon on top and bake for 20 minutes, basting frequently with the remaining sherry.

In the meantime cook the wild rice as per package instructions and cook asparagus as directed, while you heat two dinner plates on top of the stove. Place each bird on a plate, dish up rice, pour drippings from baking dish over, and serve the asparague tossed in melted butter and sprinkled with a little nutmeg. Need I say this calls for candlelight, your best lace tablecloth, and a chilled bottle of vin rosé?

If you want to go all out in your attack, follow this with:

BRANDIED STRAWBERRY WHIP
(2-3 Servings)

> 1 box strawberries, washed and hulled
> 1 - 2 tbsp. sugar
> 1/2 cup heavy cream, whipped
> 1 - 2 tbsp. brandy

Wash and hull the strawberries; whip the cream with sugar until very stiff, flavor with brandy, toss strawberries in this, and chill until ready to serve.

After this your fellow may just add further importance to the old nursery rhyme:

The Thirty Minute Dinner

Curlylocks, curlylocks,
Wilt thou be mine?
Thou shalt not wash dishes
Nor yet feed the swine,
But sit on a cushion
And sew a fine seam,
And feed upon strawberries,
Sugar and cream.

FRANK-FURTERS

Tolstoi, who once said, "If you want to be happy, be," also wrote: "Many men are like unto sausages: whatever you stuff them with, that they will bear in them." Ambrose Bierce, the American satirist, defined a lawsuit as: "A machine which you go into as a pig and come out of as a sausage."

Always a stauch supporter of the hot dog at the beach or at a ball game, I found in writing this book that it also comes in very handy when wanting to create quick, tasty, and thrifty dishes.

Certainly aware that you may already have some very good ways of fixing frankfurters, I do hope that the following pages will give you some more ideas; and should you have any qualms about serving frankfurters for dinner, just remember that it says in the Bible: "Better is a dinner of herbs where love is, than a stalled ox and hatred therewith."

This first recipe combines two of the most popular foods in the United States—the frankfurter and chili beans—so on a scale of from one to ten it should rate pretty high, aptly illustrating Victor Hugo's statement: "Popularity? It is glory's small change."

FRANKFURTER CHILE
(3-4 Servings)

1 lb. frankfurters, cut in bite-size pieces
1 large onion, chopped
1 large green pepper, chopped
4 tbsp. butter or margarine
1 tsp. salt
1/4 tsp. black pepper
1 No. 2 1/2 can tomatoes
1 tbsp. chili powder or *to taste*
1 tsp. ground coriander
1 tsp. sweet basil
1 beef bouillon cube
1 No. 303 can kidney beans

While the butter or margarine is melting in a medium-sized saucepan chop the onion and green pepper and saute in this for about 5 minutes, under cover, sprinkled with salt and pepper. Stir in the tomatoes, chili powder, coriander, and sweet basil, together with the bouillon cube. Bring to a boil, reduce heat, and let simmer for about 10 minutes before adding the kidney beans. Continue simmering for another 10 minutes, and then add the frankfurters, cut up, and let heat through. Five minutes later you should be ready to serve. Have some sourdough bread on hand, as well as foaming glasses of beer, and extra chopped onion for those who might like to sprinkle that on top.

NOTES

Being an avid fan of thick soups, I hope this next chowder recipe will become one of your favorites too, reminding you of Shakespeare's line, "The air nimbly and sweetly recommends itself unto our gentle senses."

FRANKFURTER CHOWDER
(4-6 Servings)

1 lb. frankfurters, in bite-size pieces
1 large onion, chopped
1 green pepper, seeded and chopped
2 - 3 stalks celery, diced
2 - 3 tbsp. butter or margarine
1/2 tsp. thyme
1/4 tsp. caraway seed
1/2 tsp. marjoram
1 - 2 tsp. salt
1/2 tsp. black pepper
3 cups boiling water
1 cup milk
1 12-oz. can beer
4 beef bouillon cubes
1 16-oz. can tomatoes
2 15-oz. cans precooked dry beans

While you're melting the butter or margarine in the bottom of a large pot, chop the onion, celery, and green pepper, and saute in melted butter, sprinkled with thyme, caraway seed, and marjoram, plus the salt and pepper, for about 5 minutes, under cover. When onion is limp and translucent, pour in the beans and tomatoes, together with the boiling water you started when you were through chopping vegetables, the milk, beer, and bouillon cubes. Give it a good stir, bring to a boil, reduce heat, and let simmer for about 15 to 20 minutes. Now add the frankfurters and continue simmering for another 5 minutes, or until the bite-size pieces of frankfurters are heated through. Have some sourdough rolls and beer ready to serve along with this nourishing dish that only needs fresh fruit for dessert.

Cervantes once said, "The best sauce in the world is hunger," so when you fix this next recipe make sure your guests are hungry, because it's a lot heartier than it appears on paper.

FRANKFURTER CORNBAKE
(4 Servings)

1 lb. frankfurters, cut in halves lengthwise
1 1-lb. can cream-style corn
1 cup biscuit mix
1 egg, beaten
2 tbsp. melted butter or margarine
1 tsp. salt
1/4 tsp. dry mustard
1/2 cup milk
1/2 tsp. thyme
1 4-oz. can green chiles, sliced
1/2 lb. Jack cheese, thinly sliced
Chives—*optional*

In a small saucepan melt the butter or margarine and set the oven at 450°. In a bowl mix the corn, biscuit mix, egg, and milk with melted butter or margarine, plus the salt, mustard, and thyme. Blend well before pouring half of batter into a greased 8 in. x 8 in. ovenproof dish. Now arrange the sliced chiles on top of this, following up with a layer of frankfurter halves, topped by the thinly sliced Jack cheese. Pour remaining batter over all, sprinkle chives on top if you're using them, and bake for 20 minutes. Sliced tomatoes, marinated in an oil-and-vinegar dressing, both look and taste good with this, and all you need for dessert is fresh fruit.

NOTES

Everytime I start out trying to be thrifty I unfortunately soon find myself enveloped in guilt, and like one of the characters in Shakespeare's *Hamlet* says: "My stronger guilt defeats my strong intent"; which means to me that I add a touch of costly glamour to my economy menu. You don't have to follow in my footsteps, but to test your strength I will include a recipe for dessert with this next inexpensive dinner suggestion. As the old proverb goes, "Better a good dinner than a fine coat."

FRANKFURTER RISOTTO
(4 Servings)

1 lb. frankfurters, in bite-size pieces
2 1/2 cups boiling water
1 med. onion, diced
2 - 3 stalks of celery, diced
2 med. tomatoes, in wedges
4 tbsp. butter or margarine
1/2 tsp. marjoram
1/4 tsp. caraway seed
3 beef bouillon cubes
1 tsp. salt
1/2 tsp. black pepper
1 cup raw rice
1 8-oz. can whole kernel corn, drained
Parmesan cheese

In a kettle bring some water to boil while you melt the butter or margarine in a medium-sized saucepan and dice your onion and celery stalks. Let the two vegetables sauté in melted butter or margarine for about 5 minutes, under cover, before adding the tomatoes you've cut in wedges, the marjoram, caraway seed, bouillon cubes, salt, and pepper. Pour 2 1/2 cups boiling water over, give it a good stir and when everything boils, add the raw rice, stir once more, reduce heat, and let simmer, under cover, for 15 minutes. Now add the frankfurter pieces and crained corn, stir and continue simmering under cover for another 10 minutes. Serve right out of the pot, with Parmesan cheese on the side for those who like that sprinkled on top. A glass of beer and a crisp green salad are not to be sneezed at either, unless you prefer to spend your time and money on this dreamy dessert:

PRUNE MOUND
(4 Servings)

1 12-oz. pkg. cooked, pitted prunes
1 8-oz. can almond paste
1/4 cup dry sherry
1/2 cup cream, whipped

Soak the prunes for about 10 minutes in sherry, turning once or twice to make sure every prune gets its share. With a teaspoon make little "pits" out of the almond paste and insert in the prunes after you've taken them out of the sherry. Pile stuffed prunes up on a pretty platter, dribble remaining sherry over them, whip cream stiff, and cover mound with this. Chill until ready to serve.

158 The Thirty Minute Dinner

I am a staunch believer in the importance of colors in the food you serve, and although Matthew Henry might have been right when he wrote, "Many a dangerous temptation comes to us in gay, fine colours, that are but skin-deep"; I feel *that* depth is worth taking into consideration. The next recipe should be a good example of that.

FRANKFURTER PACIFICA
(4 Servings)

1 lb. frankfurters
2 - 3 tbsp. butter or margarine
1 green pepper, seeded and cut in strips
2 med. tomatoes, in wedges
1/2 tsp. curry powder
1 12-oz. can pineapple chunks
1 1-lb. can sweet potatoes
3 tbsp. brown sugar
1 4-oz. can Chinese noodles
Parsley

Set oven at 375°. In baking dish and over low heat melt the butter or margarine while you seed and cut the green pepper into strips and wash and wedge the tomatoes. Sauté the vegetables for about 5 minutes, under cover, sprinkled with the curry powder, stirring once or twice to make sure everything is coated with butter. Drain the pineapple chunks, saving the liquid, and cut the drained sweet potatoes into chunks. Slash each of the frankfurters in two or three places in a diagonal pattern with a sharp knife. Now remove the vegetable mixture from the heat, arrange pineapple chunks, sweet potatoes, and frankfurters on top of the sauteed vegetables, blend the brown sugar with the reserved pineapple liquid, and pour over. Cover dish and bake for 25 minutes, accompanied by Chinese noodles heated along for the last 5 minutes. Parsley sprinkled on top of the franks gives the dish an even more appetizing look.

Since this is the kind of dish that could stand a solid dessert, and since you do have the oven going, why not try this next recipe, dreamed up by the young wife whose husband usually takes care of the main course while she excels in desserts.

LIZ' DATE PUDDING
(4 Servings)

1/3 cup butter or margarine
1/3 cup sugar
1/3 cup milk
1 cup flour
3/4 tsp. baking powder
1/2 cup dates, pitted and chopped
1 tbsp. butter or margarine
2 cups boiling water
1 tsp. vanilla
1 cup sugar

The Thirty Minute Dinner

If you're not already fixing the Frankfurter Pacifica set the oven at 375° and put your water on to boil. In a bowl cream the 1/3 cup butter or margarine with the 1/3 cup sugar, while in another you fix the flour with baking powder and chopped dates. Now alternating, add dry ingredients and milk to the creamed sugar, stirring well after each addition. Grease an ovenproof dish—preferably Pyrex is you have it—and pour your batter into this. By now your water should be boiling. In one of the bowls you've already used, mix the boiling water with the remaining 1 tbsp. butter or margarine and the 1 cup sugar as well as the vanilla extract. Stir well and pour over batter in dish...*do not stir!* Bake in oven for 25 to 30 minutes until golden brown on top. For some mysterious reason which I do not understand, the two layers change place, which is why you must not stir them beforehand. Serve warm.

This last recipe lends itself very well to a chilly evening so imaginately described by John Keats in his "The Eve of Saint Agnes":

> St. Agnes' Eve—Ah, bitter chill it was!
> The owl, for all his feathers, was a-cold.
> The hare limp'd trembling through the frozen grass,
> And silent was the flock in woolly fold.

If you, like I, can feel the frost biting your fingers and see the animals' steaming breaths, this next German-inspired stew will take the chill out of your bones and the evening.

FRANKFURTER SAUERKRAUT STEW
(4 Servings)

1 lb. frankfurters
4 tbsp. butter or margarine, melted
3 med. cooking apples,
    cored and diced
1 1-lb. can potatoes, drained
1 8-oz. can mushroom pieces, drained
3 cups canned sauerkraut
1/4 cup beer *or* water
3 tbsp. brown sugar
1 tsp. caraway seed
1/2 tsp. celery seed
1 tsp. salt
1/4 tsp. white pepper

While the butter is melting in a small skillet, mix together in a medium-sized saucepan the cored and diced apples with the drained potatoes, mushrooms, and sauerkraut. Blend beer or water, sugar, herbs, and spices into melted butter and pour over sauerkraut mixture before you arrange the frankfurters on top of it all, having given the frankfurters a slash or two to prevent them from popping. Cover and cook for about 20 to 25 minutes over medium heat, until everything is heated through, making sure it doesn't scorch.

Serve with pickles on the side and some good delicatessen rye bread with sweet butter...plus beer for those who want. For dessert all you will need is a cup of good coffee and some of your favorite candy.

If these recipes haven't convinced you that the frankfurter is a proper dinner dish, listen to the advice Washington Irving offered more than a hundred years ago: "How convenient it would be to many of our great men and great families of doubtful origin, could they have the privilege of the heroes of yore, who, whenever their origin was involved in obscurity, modestly announced themselves descended from a god."

LAMB

As a child I can remember reading over and over a verse by Walter de la Mare:

> *It's a very odd thing—*
> *As odd as can be—*
> *That whatever Miss T. eats*
> *Turns into Miss T.*
> *Porridge and apples,*
> *Mince, muffins and mutton,*
> *Jam, junket, jumbles—*
> *Not a rap, not a button*
> *It matters; the moment*
> *They're out of her plate,*
> *Though shared by Miss Butcher*
> *and sour Mr. Bate,*
> *Tiny and cheerful,*
> *And neat as can be,*
> *Whatever Miss T. eats*
> *Turns into Miss T.*

I wondered if my extreme fondness for mutton and lamb eventually would render me woolly all over . . . a fact I don't think would have kept me from partaking of this delicious meat. In preparing this book I was more than delighted when I discovered that it would be possible for me to include several recipes using lamb . . . in ways I hope as intriguing to you as they are to me. The first recipe is quite a variation of the standard lamb chop. If you want to use it for company—since here it is given for two—just double or triple the ingredients; it doesn't alter the cooking time. Also, since the chops have sort of a party air and since you've got the oven going, I have included a Danish Cherry Pie in the menu that you can fix while the chops are baking, and finish while you serve the chops . . . what could be more convenient?

CHEESY LAMB CHOP BAKE
(2 Servings)

4 1-in. thick rib lamb chops
2 tbsp. butter or margarine
1 tsp. salt
1/2 tsp. black pepper
1/2 tsp. thyme
2 bunches green onions, diced, tops and all
1/2 cup grated Parmesan cheese
1 cup half-and-half
1 pkg. herb rice
Water

Set oven at 400°. Melt the butter or margarine in a skillet while you sprinkle lamb chops with salt and pepper. Brown chops quickly over fairly high heat on both sides while you generously butter a small, ovenproof dish. Place browned chops in this, sprinkle thyme on top, and cover chops with diced scallions. Pour drippings from skillet over before you dust chops with Parmesan cheese and add half-and-half. Cover dish and bake for 25 minutes while you cook the herb rice according to package instructions.

Serve with a nice, crisp green salad and a bottle of chilled white wine. To keep the festive mood try this:

DANISH CHERRY PIE
(4-6 Servings)

1/2 cup butter or margarine
1 cup fine dry bread crumbs
1 tsp. cinnamon
1 8-in. prepared graham cracker pie crust
1 cup cottage cheese
1 1-lb. can cherries, drained
1 small can pineapple tidbits, drained
1 cup heavy cream, whipped
2 tbsp. sugar
1/2 tsp. vanilla extract

If you don't already have the oven set at 400°, do so. Now melt the butter in a small skillet, add cinamon and bread crumbs, and let get brown, stirring now and then while you spread the cottage cheese in bottom of pie crust, arrange the drained cherries on top of this, and sprinkle with pineapple tidbits. Spread the crumb mixture on top and bake for 15 minutes. Serve warm topped with cream you've whipped stiff and flavored with sugar and vanilla extract. If you have some left over . . . don't worry, you'll find it makes a divine snack at any hour of the day.

NOTES

It is one of those days when you're really rushed for time, yet you want to make something special for your fellow without going overboard on the budget. Either of the next two main recipes should come in handy then. Incidentally, the Greek chicken soup I have included in the Island Lamb Chop menu complements the Lamp Chop Skillet equally well, should you suddenly find yourself with an extra guest and worried about whether you have enough; just double the ingredients called for in the soup. In either case start the soup before you fix the main dish.

ISLAND LAMB CHOPS
(2 Servings)

4 rib lamb chops, 1-in. thick
2 - 3 tbsp. butter or margarine
1/2 tsp. salt
1/4 tsp. white pepper
1/2 tsp. dried mint
1 8-oz. can or jar Hollandaise sauce
1/2 cup grated Jack cheese
1 9-oz. can sliced pineapple, drained
Parmesan cheese
Paprika
Chinese noodles

While the butter is melting in a heavy skillet, sprinkle the chops with salt, pepper, and dried mint before browning them well on both sides over medium heat—six minutes on each side will do it. While this is going on mix the Hollandaise sauce with the grated Jack cheese and warm over low heat in a small saucepan, being careful not to let it boil. When chops are brown, transfer them to an ovenproof dish—set your broiler at broil—add a little more butter or margarine to skillet, and brown your pineapple slices in this on both sides. Put on top of chops, pour heated Hollandaise sauce over, sprinkle with Parmesan and paprika, and run under broiler about 2 to 3 inches from the flame for about 4 minutes, or until nicely browned. Serve with Chinese noodles on the side.

GREEK CHICKEN SOUP
(2 Servings)

1 10-oz. can chicken broth
1 soup can water
2 tbsp. raw rice
1 egg
1 tbsp. bottled lemon juice

Mix chicken broth, water, and rice in small saucepan and let simmer under cover for about 20 minutes. Just before you're ready to serve, beat the egg well with the lemon juice, add a little of the hot broth to this and pour into the soup. Serve at once.

LAMB CHOP SKILLET STEW
(3-4 Servings)

6 shoulder lamb chops
3 tbsp. flour
1/2 tsp. seasoned salt
1/4 tsp. white pepper
1 - 2 tbsp. butter or margarine
1/2 cup water
1/2 cup dry white wine
1 beef bouillon cube
1/2 tsp. marjoram
1/2 tsp. mint
1 1-lb. can potatoes, drained
4 - 6 small carrots, sliced into 1/2-in. pieces
1 8-oz. can of peas, drained

Mix flour with seasoned salt and pepper. Melt butter or margarine in deep, heavy skillet, dip chops in flour mixture, and brown well on both sides. Pour water and wine into skillet, together with bouillon cube, marjoram, and mint. Stir, cover, and let simmer for about 10 minutes while you clean and slice the carrots. Now add those to skillet, continue simmering for another 10 minutes, and add the drained potatoes and peas. Let this heat through —it takes about 5 minutes—and serve the sourdough bread and foaming glasses of beer. If you like a thicker sauce you can make a paste of whatever flour you have left over from the chops and a little pan juice, and add this to the skillet when you put in the potatoes and peas.

Fresh fruit for dessert makes a good exclamation point for this tasty, easy stew.

172 The Thirty Minute Dinner

Benjamin Franklin once said: "In general, mankind, since the improvement of cookery, eat twice as much as nature requires." If you serve the following easy but pleasing dish, you may very well find your guests proving Mr. Franklin right once more.

LAMB PILAF
(4 Servings)

1 lb. lamb, ground
2 - 3 tbsp. butter or margarine
2 - 3 leeks, washed and sliced
1 tsp. salt
1/4 tsp. white pepper
2 beef bouillon cubes
2 med. tomatoes, in wedges
1/2 tsp. dried mint
1/2 tsp. allspice
2 cups water
1 cup raw rice

While the butter or margarine is melting in a medium-sized saucepan, wash and slice your leeks and sauté them, under cover, for about 5 minutes before you add the broken-up ground lamb. Cook this just until it loses its pink color, then add the tomatoes, together with the spices, herbs, and bouillon cubes. Pour in water, bring to a quick boil, add the rice, reduce heat, cover, and let simmer for about 25 minutes, giving the dish a good stir after about 15. Serve with marinated cucumber slices and, if you are worried some of the appetites at your table won't be satisfied, try this:

CREAM OF CELERY SOUP
(4 Servings)

2 10-oz. cans cream of celery soup
2 soup cans milk
1 tbsp. instant minced onion
2 tbsp. Parmesan cheese

Heat soup according to directions on can, but add for that special touch the instant onion and Parmesan cheese while it simmers.

This next recipe, using leftover lamb, calls for two spices you may not have on your spice shelf right now, but without them you don't really have the dish, so pick them up next time you're at the grocer's, please. They'll make all the difference in this recipe and you'll find they work well in many other things as well—for instance, a little cardamom added to your favorite dumplings is a treat and, in the words of Francis Bacon, "He that will not apply new remedies must expect new evils; for time is the greatest innovator."

INDIAN LAMB SKILLET
(3-4 Servings)

3 tbsp. butter or margarine
1/4 tsp. black pepper
1/4 tsp. ground cardamom or *to taste*
1 cup raw rice
1 tsp. salt
1 10-oz. pkg. frozen asparagus
1 cup boiling water
1 cup cream
1 - 2 cups leftover lamb, shredded
1 tsp. coriander

In a deep, heavy skillet melt the butter or margarine, stir in pepper and ground cardamom, add the rice, and cook over medium heat until the rice is golden, stirring now and then. This takes about 10 minutes. Have your boiling water ready. Now add the salt, the frozen asparagus, the boiling water, the cream, shredded lamb, and coriander. Give the dish a deserved good stir, cover, and continue simmering for 15 minutes without peeking. Serve right out of the skillet for a new taste treat. For dessert have a cheese tray, accompanied by crunchy celery stalks and crisp radishes.

NOTES

176   The Thirty Minute Dinner

Samuel Johnson once said: "Most vices may be committed very genteely: a man may debauch his friend's wife genteely: he may cheat at cards genteely." After reading that I realized I could include the following recipe, which doesn't quite make it within the allotted thirty minutes, by suggesting that you simply serve one of the soups included in other menus (see Index) first, and dinner will still be ready thirty minutes after you started.

Incidentally John Gay's thoughts on the subject of cheating were: "To cheat a man is nothing; but the woman must have fine parts indeed who cheats a woman."

SOUTH AFRICAN LAMB BAKE
(4 Servings)

1 lb. ground lamb
1 small onion, diced
2 tbsp. butter or margarine
1/2 cup crumbled stale bread
3/4 cup milk
2 tsp. curry
1 - 2 tsp. salt
1/4 tsp. white pepper
1/4 tsp. sugar
1/2 cup chutney
3 eggs
1 tbsp. bottled lemon juice
1 pkg. herb rice

Set the oven at 400°. Dice the onion and sauté in melted butter in small skillet or saucepan for about 5 minutes, under cover, while you crumble the stale bread into a fairly large mixing bowl, blending it with 1/2 cup of the milk, the curry, salt, pepper, and sugar. To this add the ground lamb, together with one of the eggs, the lemon juice, chopped chutney, and onion mixture. Mix it all very well before spooning into a greased 2-qt. ovenproof dish. Bake for 20 minutes while you cook the packaged rice as per instructions. Now beat the 2 remaining eggs with the 1/4 cup of milk you have left and pour over mixture in baking dish. Continue baking for another 15 minutes and serve with the rice on the side . . . and more chutney for those who like this delightful condiment.

I've never been to South Africa where this dish comes from, but that does not prevent me from dreaming up all sorts of pictures when I serve it, drawing on books I've read and pictures I've seen . . . and most of all . . . remembering the words of Anatole France, "To know is nothing at all; to imagine is everything."

PORK

Did you know that the pig was once made the subject of serious mathematical studies and that Vauban, a 19th-century slide-rule expert, figured out that over a period of twelve years a single sow would deliver 6,434,838 piglets? That would have to be with the help of children, grandchildren and great grandchildren . . . but no wonder that bacon became such a popular breakfast dish.

Pork was also the main source of nourishment for the Gauls, and the ancient Romans cooked them whole. One medieval Grimod de la Reyniere eulogized the pig, saying in part: "He is the king of the unclean beasts. His empire is the most universal and his qualities less contested than any other. Without him, no bacon, and therefore no cooking; without him, no ham, no sausage, no black puddings. Foolish physicians! You condemn the pig, and his indigestibility is one of the finest ornaments in your crown! What ingratitude has permitted his name to become a word of opprobrium?"

That's quite a stirring speech even if I did have to look up that last word to find out that it means the disgrace that follows shameful conduct.

With such a historical background I didn't dare not set out in search of recipes using this noble but apparently much maligned animal, and knew I had hit the jackpot when I discovered the many uses one can put the precooked ham to. On the following pages you will see what I mean.

Aside from using ham as their meaty base, the recipes have one more thing in common—they're all enhanced by the accompaniment of a glass of cold beer. As Edward Fitzgerald wrote:

> *Ah, fill the Cup:—what boots it to repeat*
> *How time is slipping underneath our feet:*
> *Unborn tomorrow, and dead Yesterday,*
> *Why fret about them if Today be sweet.*

CURRIED HAM PILAF
(3-4 Servings)

1 lb. precooked ham, cubed
1 large onion, diced
1 green pepper, seeded and cut in strips
3 med. tomatoes, cut in wedges
4 tbsp. butter or margarine
1 - 2 tsp. salt

1/2 tsp. pepper
1/2 tsp. dill weed
1 cup raw rice
2 cups boiling water
1 - 2 tsp. curry powder

Start boiling your water and melt the butter or margarine in a dish you can carry right to the table, while you chop the onion and clean and slice the green pepper. Sauté onion and pepper for about 5 minutes in butter, under cover, during which time you cube the ham, wedge the tomatoes, and measure out your other ingredients. When the onion is limp and translucent, add the ham together with tomatoes, salt, pepper, and dill; pour the boiling water over all, bring to a quick second boil, stir in the raw rice together with the curry, reduce heat, and let simmer for 15 minutes, before you give it another stir and continue simmering for another 10 minutes or until liquid is more or less absorbed; serve with this easily fixed:

CHEESE BREAD
(4 Servings)

8 slices of white bread
Butter or margarine
8 slices of Swiss cheese
Paprika

Set oven at 400°. Butter the sliced bread, top with cheese, sprinkle with paprika and bake for 5 minutes... *voilà*, a little special touch added to your dinner.

Emerson once said, "There's always a best way of doing everything, even if it be to boil an egg." I hope the next recipe meets with his . . . and your . . . approval.

CURRIED HAM AND EGG BAKE
(4 Servings)

    1 lb. precooked ham, cubed
    8 eggs
    1 med. onion, chopped
    2 tbsp. butter or margarine
    1 tbsp. flour
    4 tbsp. butter or margarine
    1 1/2 cups chicken broth
    1 cup heavy cream
    1 tsp. salt or to taste
    2 tsp. curry
    1/8 tsp. white pepper
    1/4 cup fine bread crumbs
    1 4-oz. can shoestring potatoes

While you're hard-boiling the eggs . . . this takes about 12 to 15 minutes . . . melt in an ovenproof dish the 2 tbsp. butter or margarine and sauté your chopped onion and cubed ham in this, under cover, over low heat. Set your oven at 375°. Get out a medium-sized saucepan; in this melt the 4 tbsp. butter or margarine, add the flour, let brown, and then stir in chicken broth, cream, salt, pepper, and curry. Cook over low heat until fairly thick; this takes about 5 minutes. Give the onion-and-ham mixture a stir and grease an oven-proof dish lavishly. By now your eggs should be done. Shell them under running, cold water and cut in halves. Pour ham-onion mixture into bottom of baking dish, top with egg halves, and pour curry sauce over all. Sprinkle with bread crumbs, dot with a little extra butter or margarine, and run under broiler for about 3 minutes or until golden brown. Serve with shoestring potatoes you've heated for about 5 minutes in the oven, and remember, the canned variety is rather salty, so go easy on the salt in the main dish.

Have some fresh fruit dessert and you will have no complaints.

This next recipe from the Far East uses a vegetable ordinarily left out of cooking—the radish. Why more use is not made of this tasty root, I don't know. I'd hate to think it was the reason the late Ed Wynn gave for selling his farm: "Every radish I ever pulled up seemed to have a mortgage attached to it."

FAR EASTERN HAM AND RICE
(4 Servings)

1 lb. precooked ham, cubed
1 med. onion, chopped
2 tbsp. butter or margarine
2 cups boiling water
1/4 cup soy sauce
2 chicken bouillon cubes
1 tsp. salt
1/4 tsp. white pepper
1/4 tsp. dry mustard or to taste
1 cup raw rice
1/2 cup raisins
8 large radishes, sliced
Chutney
Salted peanuts

Start boiling your water; while in a medium-sized saucepan you melt the butter or margarine. Chop the onion, add to butter and sauté, under cover, for 5 minutes. Now add the boiling water, soy sauce, bouillon cubes, salt, pepper, and mustard, together with the raw rice. Give it all a good stir and as soon as it boils reduce heat and let simmer for about 15 minutes, while you cube the ham, slice the radishes, and get the condiments ready. After 15 minutes add the ham and raisins, and in another 5 minutes the radishes. Simmer for another 5 minutes or so and serve with chutney and salted peanuts on the side. A glass of beer is a must with this dish... and should you worry about the more sturdy appetites at your table, why not have the elegant soup first?

WINE CONSOMMÉ
(3-4 Servings)

2 10-oz. cans consommé
1/2 soup can water
1/2 tsp. crumbled bay leaves
1/2 cup dry red wine

Let the soup, water, and bay leaves simmer for about 5 minutes before you add the wine. Heat through, but do not boil. Skim top with a paper towel to catch stray herbs, and serve in delicate china soup bowls.

188 The Thirty Minute Dinner

Aside from being tasty this next recipe is also very economical and a great hit with the kids. If you're the happy owner of a boat, it has the added advantage of staying on your plate, no matter how much the galley rolls.

HAM, CHEESE, AND POTATO BAKE
(4 Servings)

1 pkg. instant mashed potatoes (for 4)
Water
Milk
Butter or margarine
1/4 tsp. caraway seed
1/4 tsp. dry mustard
1 lb. precooked ham, cubed
1/2 cup heavy cream, whipped
1 cup grated Cheddar cheese
1/4 tsp. dill weed

Set oven at 450° and prepare instant mashed potatoes according to package instructions adding caraway seed and mustard to the water. Grease a baking dish generously and spoon the mashed potatoes into the bottom. Arrange the cubed ham on top, whip the cream, sprinkled with dill weed, and gently fold the grated Cheddar cheese into this before spreading on top of ham. Bake for about 10 to 15 minutes and serve with a crisp, green salad and glasses of beer for those who are old enough.

All you will need for dessert is fresh fruit.

In describing political opponents Samuel Johnson once said: "A wise Tory and a wise Whig, I believe, will agree. Their principles are the same, though their modes of thinking are different." The principle for this next recipe is the same as above, but the outcome quite different and rather appealing.

HAM-VEGETABLE BAKE
(3-4 Servings)

1 lb. precooked ham, cubed
1 med. onion, chopped
2 large potatoes, peeled
  and very thinly sliced
4 lettuce leaves, shredded
2 - 3 tbsp. butter or margarine
1/2 tsp. thyme
1/4 tsp. chervil
1 tsp. salt
1 8-oz. can peas, drained
1 cup heavy cream
1/2 cup grated Cheddar cheese

Set the oven at 375°. Chop the onion and peel and slice the potatoes very thin...the wide slot on your grater is ideal for this. In an ovenproof dish melt the butter or margarine on the top of the stove and let the onion, potato, and lettuce leaves, sprinkled with herbs and salt, sauté in this for about 5 minutes, covered to keep the moisture

190 The Thirty Minute Dinner

in. While this is being done, cube the ham, drain the peas, and grate the cheese. When the onion and potato slices are translucent, add ham and peas to dish, give it a stir before you pour the cream in, and sprinkle the cheese on top. Bake, covered, for about 20 minutes and serve with hard-crust dinner rolls you've heated along during the last 10 minutes of baking time.

A piece of chocolate cake from your favorite pastry shop makes a nice dessert.

As much as I adore Edward Lear and his limericks, I must take exception to the character described in this sample of his fun poetry:

> *There was an old person of Dean,*
> *Who dined on one pea and one bean*
> *For he said: "More than that,*
> *Would make me too fat,"*
> *That cautious old person of Dean.*

I mean, who could make a meal out of one pea and one bean? I certainly can't, so let me offer you a more generous version of the popular baked bean dish.

HAMMY BAKED BEANS
(4 Servings)

1 lb. precooked ham, cubed
2 small onions, thinly sliced
1 - 2 tbsp. butter or margarine
2 1-lb. cans baked beans
1/4 cup dark brown sugar, firmly packed
2 tbsp. pickle relish
1/2 tsp. dry mustard or to taste
1/4 tsp. cinnamon
1/4 tsp. black pepper
1/2 cup grated Cheddar cheese

Set your oven at 350° and sauté the sliced onion and cubed ham in the melted butter or margarine for about 5 minutes, under cover. In the meantime grease a 2-qt. baking dish and get all the other ingredients ready. When onions are limp and translucent pour onion-ham mixture into baking dish, mix well with all other ingredients, except cheese—really stirring it around—sprinkle cheese on top, and bake, uncovered, for 20 minutes. Serve with sourdough rolls and have some chopped Bermuda onions on hand for those who like to mix that up with their beans. And who has ever heard of serving baked beans without beer?

If you really want to disregard that old person from Dean in Lear's limerick, why don't you try this easy dessert:

CHOCOLATE PINEAPPLE RINGS
(4 Servings)

1 1-lb. can pineapple rings,
   well drained
2 squares sweet baking chocolate,
   grated
1/4 cup mint-flavored liqueur

While you're draining the pineapple rings well, melt the grated chocolate in a small saucepan with the liqueur, and lightly grease a piece of waxed paper. Dip the individual rings of pineapple into chocolate mixture, making sure they're coated on both sides, and let them dry or harden on the wax paper before serving.

Hardly anyone has praised the value of companionship when eating better than Jonathan Swift when he said: "He showed me his bill of fare to tempt me to dine with him; poh, said I, I value not your bill of fare, give me your bill of company." But in spite of this I think most of us try to go a little out of our way when we expect company. This next recipe doesn't have to take a back seat to any company fare.

HAMMY GREEN PEPPERS
(3-4 Servings)

1 lb. precooked ham, cubed
4 - 6 green peppers, seeded and thinly sliced
1 med. large onion, thinly sliced
4 tbsp. butter or margarine
2 tbsp. water
1/2 tsp. meat sauce (Maggi, Bovril, etc.)
1 tsp. salt
1/4 tsp. white pepper
1/4 tsp. fennel seed
1 cup grated Swiss cheese

While the butter or margarine is melting in a deep, large skillet, slice the peppers and onion and let them sauté for about 5 minutes, before adding the water, meat sauce, salt, pepper, and fennel seed. Cook over high heat for about 10 minutes, stirring frequently to prevent scorching. When the onion is slightly brown, add the cubed

194 The Thirty Minute Dinner

ham and grated cheese and continue cooking over medium heat for another 5 minutes before you serve, accompanied by sliced, marinated tomatoes and hard-crust dinner rolls.

A piece of cheesecake puts a nice period to this meal.

NOTES

A friend of mine lived in Samoa for two years and returned to the mainland hopelessly in love with the Samoans and their way of life

Not only do the Samoans seem to be one of the few groups that live according to this thought from Oscar Wilde: "As long as war is regarded as wicked, it will always have its fascination. When it is looked upon as vulgar, it will cease to be popular." The Samoans do exactly that. They also have an enormous talent for turning any crisis into a hilarious joke—a talent that sure comes in handy for the housewife when she is racing the clock.

Another trait that fascinated her was their tribal discipline. The two-year-olds mind the four-year-olds, the four-year-olds mind the six-year-olds, and so on up the line, making the generation gap a nonexistent problem. They live in large "families" with everybody contributing their earnings to the welfare of the whole family . . . and with this sliding rule of authority nobody gets away with shedding his responsibility.

The only time she saw some downcast, unhappy eyes was when it came time to slaughter the village pigs. With a life-style that at best can be described as informal, the household pig could easily become a pet . . . a fact that could put a damper on the occasion . . . but the Samoans honored the pig by turning it into dishes that would be talked about for a long time. This next recipe is a good example.

SAMOAN PORK AND VEGETABLES
(4 Servings)

2 lbs. pork tenderloin
2 - 3 tbsp. butter or margarine
2 - 3 scallions, minced
1/2 tsp. curry powder
1 tsp. thyme
1/4 tsp. nutmeg
1/4 tsp. black pepper
2/3 cup dry Vermouth

Have your butcher slice the tenderloin into 3/4 in. thick fillets. In a deep skillet melt the butter or margarine and brown the pork well on both sides, keeping an eye on it while you mince the scallions, making sure the meat doesn't scorch. Turn down the heat when meat is brown, add the scallions, spices, and herbs, and continue to simmer, under cover, for 10 minutes, before you add the vermouth. Give everything a good stir and continue simmering for another 10 minutes while you fix the vegetables to go with it . . . and don't worry . . . the pork will be cooked through by the time you serve.

DELECTABLE VEGETABLES
(4 Servings)

1 1-lb. can small onions, drained
1 tbsp. liquid honey
1 10-oz. pkg. frozen artichoke hearts
1 1-lb. can carrots, drained
1 tsp. salt
1/2 tsp. seasoned salt
1/4 tsp. pepper
1/4 tsp. allspice
1/2 tsp. dill weed
2 - 3 tbsp. butter or margarine

Drain the onions and pour into small bowl; cover them with the liquid honey, stirring until they're well coated. In a medium-sized saucepan, with cover, melt the butter or margarine, add all the vegetables, including the honeyed onions, the herbs, and spices, stir well and simmer, under cover, over medium-low heat for about 8 minutes . . . and no, I didn't forget to add any liquid. The juices from the vegetables themselves will take care of that.

To save on dishes serve meat right out of the skillet with the vegetables being ladled out of their saucepan. All you need to top this off are some hard-crust dinner rolls and a nice bottle of vin rosé, chilled.

It was Dickens who once said, "It is a melancholy truth that even great men have their poor relations." However, this Hawaiian cousin of the Samoan pork dish needn't feel badly about that. It has enough distinction to stand on its own merit . . . and it doesn't need your constant attention.

HAWAIIAN PORK SKILLET
(3-4 Servings)

1 lb. lean pork, in strips
1 med. onion, chopped
1 green pepper, seeded and diced
1/2 tsp. sweet basil
2 - 3 tbsp. butter or margarine
3 tbsp. flour
1 cup dry white wine
1 8-oz. can pineapple chunks, (reserve liquid)
1/4 cup chutney, chopped
1/2 tbsp. curry powder or *to taste*
1/2 tsp. salt
1/4 tsp. black pepper
1 4-oz. can shoestring potatoes

Cut the lean pork in thin strips, chop the onion, and dice the green pepper, starting to melt your butter or margarine when you are about halfway through taking care of these details. Now sauté these three items, sprinkled with sweet basil, in the butter for about 5 minutes, under cover. Sprinkle flour in and gradually stir in white wine and the syrup you have reserved from the pineapple chunks. Bring mixture to a boil, add the chopped chutney, curry, salt, and pepper; reduce heat and simmer, under cover, for 10 minutes before you add the pineapple chunks. Let those just heat through and you're ready to serve with shoestring potatoes on the side . . . but remember, the canned ones are pretty salty, so allow for that in tasting for salt.

Assorted cheeses make a nice follow-up to this unusual pork dish. Incidentally, did you know what Jonathan Swift's definition of bachelor fare is? "Bread, and cheese, and kisses"—a definition that should carry over to the dessert for the following recipe as well, being something on the sweet side as it is.

SWEET AND SOUR PORK
(4 Servings)

1 lb. lean pork, cut into thin strips
2 1/2 cups boiling water
1/4 cup cornstarch
1/2 cup cider vinegar
1/4 cup brown sugar, firmly packed
2 tbsp. soy sauce
2 tbsp. butter or margarine
1/2 tsp. dry mustard
1 10-oz. pkg. frozen peas
1 10-oz. pkg. frozen cauliflower
2 stalks celery, in 1-in. pieces
1 tsp. salt—*optional*
9 9-oz. can pineapple slices, drained
1/4 cup toasted almonds
Chinese noodles

While you bring the water to a boil in a saucepan, blend cornstarch with vinegar into a smooth paste; slowly add this to boiling water, followed by sugar and soy sauce. Reduce heat and cook, stirring occasionally, until thickened and transparent. In the meantime, melt the butter or margarine in a large, deep skillet, sprinkle with mustard, and let it blend with butter before you brown in it the pork you've cut into thin strips. Break the frozen peas and cauliflower into meat mixture, together with sliced celery, sprinkle with salt if you think you need it, pour cornstarch mixture over all, and let simmer for 20 minutes, under cover. Just before you're ready to serve add the drained pineapple slices, let heat through, and sprinkle with toasted almonds, done in a slow oven during the last 5 minutes. Serve with Chinese noodles on the side and engage in happy conversation at the table because, as you can tell, you won't have time during the preparation of this dish.

If you're as much of a meat loaf fan as I am, try this next recipe, hailing from Denmark where they really do know what to do with pork.

PORKY MEAT LOAF
(3-4 Servings)

1 lb. lean pork, ground
1 lb. precooked ham, ground
2 eggs, beaten
1 cup fine, dry breadcrumbs
1 cup commercial sour cream
1 tbsp. bottled lemon juice
1-2 tsp. instant minced onion
1 tsp. curry powder
1 tsp. ginger
1/2 tsp. dry mustard
1/4 tsp. nutmeg
1-2 tsp. salt
1/2 tsp. black pepper
1 1-lb. can potatoes, drained
Parsley
Butter or margarine

Set oven at 350°. In a large bowl mix together the pork and ham, which you've had your butcher run through the grinder twice, with all the other ingredients, except canned potatoes. Before shaping into three mini-loaves, make sure everything is well blended. Lightly grease an ovenproof dish and bake loaves for 25 minutes.

Now for the sauce that goes over at the last minute:

1/2 cup water
1 cup cider vinegar
1 tbsp. bottled lemon juice
1 cup brown sugar
1 tsp. dry mustard

Mix all the above ingredients together in a small saucepan and let simmer for about 10 minutes. A couple of minutes before you are ready to serve, and after you've started the drained potatoes sautéing in about 1 or 2 tbsp. butter or margarine in a small covered saucepan, pour sauce over meat loaves and let blend with pan juices for a couple of minutes.

Serve with the potatoes tossed with parsley, and make sure you have some delicatessen rye and cold beer on hand as well; both are absolutely musts with this splendid treat.

You have promised them homemade spaghetti, but suddenly all the time is gone. You were about to try and sneak the canned variety over on them, when you saw the glimpse of disappointment on their faces and no longer could live up to Oliver Goldsmith's thought: "As for disappointing them I should not so much mind; but I can't abide to disappoint myself." Don't worry . . . you can please everyone with this next recipe. It's fixed in a jiffy yet has that homemade appeal.

PORKY SPAGHETTI
(4-6 Servings)

1 lb. pork sausage
1/2 lb. ground beef
1 large onion, chopped
1/4 tsp. garlic powder
1/2 tsp. thyme
1/4 tsp. ground cumin
2 8-oz. cans tomato sauce
1 4-oz. can mushroom pieces
1 tbsp. Worcestershire sauce
1 tsp. salt
1/2 tsp. black pepper
2 cups grated Cheddar cheese
1 8-oz. pkg. spaghetti

Chop the onion and break up the pork sausage and ground beef before you brown them in a large, deep skillet. Sprinkle with garlic powder, thyme, and cumin, stir now and then, and in about 5 minutes the beef should have lost its red color and most of the fat from the pork sausage should be rendered. Now start cooking the spaghetti according to package instructions, while you pour off excess grease from skillet before adding the tomato sauce, the undrained mushrooms, the Worcestershire sauce, salt, and pepper. Bring this mixture to a boil and let simmer, covered and over medium low heat, for about 15 minutes. Now add your cheese to skillet, drain the spaghetti (that should be *al dente* now) in a colander, return to its pot, pour spaghetti sauce over, and toss before serving to a happy family.

Have a green salad ready as well, but limit dessert to fresh fruit. That's all you will need.

VEAL

There really was a time when no self-respecting housewife would have entertained without serving a roast for her sit-down dinner guests—but in our age of eat-on-the run and diversified family interests, that is quickly becoming a thing of the past—as is, unfortunately, dinner conversation, so aptly described by Jonathan Swift in a poem:

> *Conversation is but carving!*
> *Give no more to every guest*
> *Than he's able to digest.*
> *Give him always of the prime,*
> *And but little at a time.*
> *Carve to all but just enough*
> *Let them neither starve nor stuff,*
> *And that you may have your due,*
> *Let your neighbor carve for you.*

The Thirty Minute Dinner

Obviously, in this book I cannot furnish you with recipes for roasts, upon which you may both practice your art of carving and your talent for conversation. But I do hope that on the following pages you will find a few more recipes that will not only intrigue you, but also please the palate of your guests and encourage them to linger at the table to engage in conversation, the success of which is based on being able to disagree without being disagreeable . . . or to put it in culinary terms, as did Charles Dudley Warner: "Lettuce is like conversation; it must be fresh and crisp, so sparkling that you scarcely notice the bitter in it."

But back to the matter at hand . . . veal. Since you're not going to buy any roasts or big pieces like that, do explain to your butcher exactly how you plan to serve or cook the veal. He'll be flattered and in return guide you to the proper cuts . . . or maybe even cut it especially for you.

AUSTRIAN VEAL SCHNITZEL
(3-4 Servings)

1 1/2 lbs. veal cutlet
4 tbsp. butter or margarine
3 tbsp. flour
1 tsp. salt
1/2 tsp. rosemary, crushed
2 tsp. paprika
1 med. onion, chopped
6 - 8 large mushrooms, washed and quartered
2 tbsp. flour

1 cup milk
1/2 tsp. crumbled bay leaves
1 cup commercial sour cream
1/2 of 1 8-oz. pkg. noodles
Butter or margarine
Caraway seed

Start cooking your noodles according to package instructions, while in a large, deep skillet you melt 3 tbsp. of the butter or margarine, and dust the veal cutlets well in the flour you've mixed with salt, crushed rosemary, and paprika. Brown veal nicely on both sides and remove to keep warm (wrapped in foil and kept in an oven set on low is the easiest way). Add remaining butter to skillet after you've chopped and sliced the onion and mushrooms. Sauté vegetables for about 5 minutes before you sprinkle them with flour and gradually stir in the milk together with the crumbled bay leaves. When sauce is thick, stir in sour cream, return veal to skillet, and let heat through, without boiling, while you drain the noodles in a colander and toss them with a little butter and caraway seed in the pot you used for them—that way you lose no heat.

Have some beer on hand in the refrigerator, and all you'll need for dessert are cookies with coffee you might flavor with a little cocoa and top with whipped cream.

This next recipe comes from Denmark where because of the climate they are somewhat limited in their choice of exotic vegetables and fruits, not to mention spices. But that doesn't faze the Danish cooks. They use very basic ingredients in a most imaginative way, proving in a roundabout way the words of Samuel Johnson: "Were it not for imagination, a man would be as happy in the arms of a chambermaid as of a Duchess."

DANISH VEAL SCHNITZEL
(3-4 Servings)

1 1/2 lbs. veal cutlets, sliced very thin
2 eggs, beaten
1/2 cup minced green onions *or* chives
1/2 cup grated Parmesan cheese
1/2 cup fine, dry bread crumbs
1/4 cup butter or margarine
1/4 cup olive oil
1 tsp. salt
1/4 tsp. white pepper
1 cup half-and-half
1/2 cup sherry or dry white wine
1 pkg. instant mashed potatoes

Have your friendly butcher slice the veal very thin for you. Start out by beating the two eggs in a small bowl and making three little piles of bread crumbs, cheese, and minced green onions, on pieces of waxed paper (to avoid the extra dishes). Now get the cutlets ready for frying by dipping them first in bread crumbs, then in beaten eggs, then in cheese, back to the eggs, and onto the green onions. When you're about halfway through with this somewhat messy job, start heating your butter or margarine and olive oil in a large, deep skillet. When you're all finished dipping, brown cutlets well over medium heat. Transfer the meat to a warm platter, cover with foil, and keep warm in low oven while you add 1 tsp. of salt and 1/4 tsp. of white pepper to the drippings in the skillet; stir well before you pour in the half-and-half and sherry, together with what green onions and cheese you may have left over. Let this simmer over low heat and under cover, while you fix the instant mashed potatoes according to instructions. Pour gravy into a small gravy boat or pitcher and serve with cutlets and mashed potatoes.

A glass of cold beer is an absolute must with this, and for dessert all you need is fresh fruit.

Milton once wrote:

> *For nothing lovelier can be found*
> *In woman, than to study household good,*
> *And good works in her husband to promote.*

A Hungarian friend of mine is a living example of this. Without any assistance from Women's Lib she's managed to carve out quite a fashion career for herself, while she assists her husband in his financial consulting business and runs a smooth household, claiming all the time she couldn't do one without the others. She is a delightful lady ... and here's one of the recipes that makes it possible for her always to look as if she had all the time in the world.

VEAL SCHNITZEL PAPRIKA
(4 Servings)

2 lbs. veal cutlets
4 tbsp. butter or margarine
4 minced green onions
1 dash salt
1 tbsp. flour
2 tsp. paprika
1/2 tsp. sweet basil
1 10-oz. can chicken broth
1/2 cup dry white wine
1/2 cup sour cream
1 - 2 tsp. bottled lemon juice
1 pkg. instant mashed potatoes
1/2 - 1 tsp. dill weed

Have the butcher cut the veal very thin. Melt the butter or margarine in a large, deep skillet and lightly brown veal in this over high heat before wrapping in foil and transferring to an oven set on low to keep it warm. Quickly mince the green onions and sauté in skillet, sprinkled with just a dash of salt, for about 5 minutes, under cover, stirring once or twice. Mix the paprika and sweet basil with the flour before sprinkling over onion mixture, stir, and start to gradually add the chicken broth and wine, cooking until thick and smooth, about 10 minutes. Fix the instant mashed potatoes according to package instructions, but add the dill weed to the water. When the sauce is through cooking, add the sour cream and lemon juice to skillet, together with the veal, and let everything heat through, but, do not boil. Serve with the mashed potatoes on the side and in front of you have a chilled glass of vin rosé . . . it's a definite plus—both in color and taste.

The Thirty Minute Dinner

Before you go out in the kitchen to fix this next recipe, set your table, because once you start the dish you have to stay with it. However, everything can be done within thirty minutes and your efforts definitely deserve a bottle of wine. We should all remember the words of Oliver Herford:

> *God made Man*
> *Frail as a bubble;*
> *God made Love*
> *Love made Trouble.*
> *God made the Vine;*
> *Was it a sin*
> *That man made Wine*
> *To drown Trouble in?*

CHEESY VEAL CUTLETS
(2-3 Servings)

1 lb. veal cutlets
2 eggs
1/4 tsp. salt
1/4 cup grated Parmesan cheese
1/2 cup dry fine bread crumbs
1 - 2 tbsp. butter or margarine
1/2 tsp. oregano
1 8-oz. can tomato sauce
4 slices Mozarella cheese
1 1-lb. can potatoes, drained
1 tbsp. butter or margarine
1 tbsp. bottled lemon juice
Parsley

Set the oven on broil. Beat the 2 eggs together with salt. Mix the Parmesan cheese with the bread crumbs and spread on a piece of waxed paper. In an ovenproof dish melt the butter or margarine, with the oregano sprinkled in, while you dip the cutlets first in eggs and then crumb-and-cheese mix. Brown veal cutlets lightly on both sides in herbed butter, pour the tomato sauce over them, and cover with Mozarella cheese. Broil 4 in. from the flame for about 6 minutes, while in a small saucepan you saute the drained potatoes in the remaining butter mixed with lemon juice. Just before you're ready to serve, toss the potatoes with parsley and have a wide spatula ready to transfer veal and lusciously melted cheese from dish to platters. Have some crusty bread on hand and if you're in the mood for a salad, sliced avocados, tossed with canned drained grapefruit sections in an oil-and-vinegar dressing make for a nice accompaniment.

To stay in the Italian mood of this dish, have spumoni for dessert.

These next two recipes also take their inspiration from Italy; you should have no qualms about serving them for company. You may even find they'll prove the point of Oscar Wilde's line: "An acquaintance that begins with a compliment is sure to develop into a real friendship."

VEAL PICCATA
(4 Servings)

1 1/2 lbs. veal, cut for scalloppini
2 tbsp. butter or margarine
2 tbsp. olive oil
1 tsp. salt
1/4 tsp. black pepper
1/4 cup dry white wine
1/4 cup beef broth *or*
1/4 cup water and 1/2 tsp. meat sauce (Maggi, Bovril, etc.)
4 tbsp. bottled lemon juice
2 lemons, sliced
1 small can anchovies
1 1-lb. can potatoes, drained
1 tbsp. butter or margarine
Parsley and Parmesan cheese
1 10-oz. pkg. frozen spinach

While you're sautéeing the covered potatoes over low, low heat in 1 tbsp. butter or margarine, and cooking the frozen spinach according to package instructions, in a skillet quickly brown the veal in 2 tbsp. butter or margarine, blended with 2 tbsp. olive oil. Sprinkle with salt and pepper, gently pour in the wine, broth, and lemon juice, and arrange the sliced lemon on top of the meat. Cover skillet and let simmer for 3-4 minutes. With a slotted spoon transfer veal to a heated platter, arrange anchovies on top of veal, while the juices simmer a little longer. Pour sauce over veal and serve with Parsley-dusted potatoes and spinach sprinkled with Parmesan cheese.

The delicate flavor of this great dish is, of course, enhanced by a glass of chilled white wine. Follow this with a piece of your favorite cheesecake—cherry-topped makes for a colorful ending—and you'll have enjoyed a truly delightful dinner.

VEAL SCALLOPS VERDE
(4 Servings)

1 1/2 lbs. veal scallops
1 tsp. salt
1 tsp. paprika
1/2 cup olive oil
1/2 cup bottled lemon juice
1/8 tsp. garlic powder
1 tsp. prepared mustard
1/4 tsp. nutmeg
1/2 tsp. sugar
4 tbsp. butter or margarine
1 med. onion, thinly sliced
1 green pepper, cut in strips
6-8 large mushrooms, washed and quartered
1/4 cup flour
1 10-oz. can of chicken broth
1/2 cup dry white wine
1 2-oz. can sliced olives
1 8-oz. pkg. spinach noodles
Parmesan cheese

While the veal, cut in serving pieces, is resting in a flat dish in a marinade you've made by throughly blending the olive oil, lemon juice, salt, paprika, garlic powder, mustard, nutmeg, and sugar, sauté in a deep skillet and under cover your sliced onion and pepper strips in half the butter, i.e. 2 tbsp., for a good 5 minutes. Start the water for your spinach noodles. Wash and quarter the mushrooms transfer with a slotted spoon the onion mixture to a plate, and let the mushrooms saute for about 4 minutes, before adding to the onion mixture you've set aside. Now lift the veal out of the marinade. Dip it in flour and quickly brown it in the remaining butter or margarine you've added to the skillet. When browned on both sides, return vegetable mixture to skillet, combine chicken broth and wine with marinade, and pour over all. Bring to a boil, reduce heat, and let simmer for about 10 minutes. Just before serving add the drained olive slices to skillet, toss the noodles (that you've drained in a colander) with a little butter, and have some Parmesan ready to pass around the table to those who would like it. A glass of vin rosé not only looks good with this, it also tastes nice.

After serving this you can rest on your laurels and just have fresh fruit for dessert.

Veal 219

The last two recipes in this chapter are sort of Mediterranean versions of our American hamburger . . . but believe me, although quite different in flavor, certain to go over with the kids. And do try the cucumber salad I have included with the Greek version. For once I must take umbrage at one of Samuel Johnson's statements, "A cucumber should be well sliced, and dressed with pepper and vinegar, and then thrown out as good for nothing!". . . but then, the mightiest can err, right?

GREEK VEAL PATTIES
(4 Servings)

1 lb. ground veal
1/2 lb. ground lamb
1/2 tsp. dried mint
1 tsp. oregano
1 - 2 tsp. salt
1/4 tsp. white pepper
2 - 3 tbsp. bottled lemon juice
3 - 4 tbsp. butter or margarine
1 pkg. saffron rice

While the rice is cooking according to package instructions, mix all the other ingredients, with the exception of the butter or margarine, in a bowl and blend well—the hands are still the best tools for this. Shape meat mixture into patties and brown well in butter or margarine, covering when brown and letting simmer, over reduced heat, until rice is done. To stay in the Greek mood accompany with this salad:

CUCUMBERS WITH YOGURT

2 cucumbers, sliced
4 green onions, diced
1/2 cup yogurt
1 tsp. sugar
1/2 tsp. salt
1/4 tsp. black pepper

Before you start dinner, slice the cucumbers very thin into a bowl and let stand in refrigerator for about 20 minutes. Just before serving mix yogurt with sugar, salt, and dice the green onions. Squeeze excess liquid from cucumbers and toss with green onions and yogurt dressing.

MEDITERRANEAN VEAL PATTIES
(4 Servings)

1 1/2 lbs. ground veal
1/2 lb. ground ham
1 tsp. salt
1/2 tsp. black pepper
1/4 tsp. lemon peel
1 egg, beaten
Bread crumbs
6 tbsp. butter or margarine
1 med. onion, diced
1 8-oz. can pitted green olives, sliced
1/2 cup dry white wine
1 8-oz. pkg. herb rice

Fix the herbed rice according to instructions. Mix together the ground veal and ham with salt, pepper, and lemon peel, while the diced onion is sautéing in 2 tbsp. of the butter or margarine for about 5 minutes. Shape meat mixture into patties, about 6 of them, push the onions aside, and brown the patties on both sides after dipping them first in the beaten egg and then the bread crumbs, adding more butter or margarine as needed. Stir sliced olives into drippings, pour the wine over, cover, and let simmer for about 15 minutes. Serve with sliced tomatoes you have marinated in an oil-and-vinegar dressing.

For dessert have some ice cream you've topped with toasted, shredded coconut . . . the latter done in a very low oven while you eat the veal patties.

VARIETY MEATS

Charles Lamb once said about himself: "I am, in plainer words, a bundle of prejudices—made up of likings and dislikings." And Somerset Maugham commented on the same subject: "I forget who it was that recommended men for their soul's good to do each day two things they disliked . . . it is a precept that I have followed scrupulously; for every day I have got up and I have gone to bed."

Mr. Maugham certainly set an example that proved prejudices can be overcome, whatever they may be, and I wish more people would try to forget some of their built-in aversions when it comes to food . . . usually foods they haven't even tasted, but for some reason have decided they don't like . . . like variety meats.

So next time you serve, say, liver or kidneys and are met with sour faces, tell your hesitant eaters that they might start considering themselves lucky . . . for a lot of reasons. You *could* be cooking from the Alexander Dumas cookbook which has a recipe for kangaroo fillets, a meat he was very interested in and thought of importing as cattle to Europe—a project he abandoned when he discovered the kangaroo had an inordinate fondness for wine and brandy.

Or you might remind them that in the Far East birds' nests, cleaned and simmered under a roasting fowl, are considered an absolute delicacy, and in other parts of the world the hostess would be delighted if she could serve such delicacies as boar's head, cockscombs, and—I kid you not—elephant's feet and whale steak. Compared to such culinary recklessness the following recipes become positively square and everyday . . . a state I would enjoy, since the so-called variety meats and the dishes they offer deserve a much wider popularity than now enjoyed. Let's hope Thomas Hood was right when he said: "There are three things which the public will always clamour for, sooner or later: namely, Novelty, Novelty, Novelty."

So please try the following recipes and see if it hasn't come time for you and your guests to enjoy something new.

CHICKEN LIVERS JARDINIÈRE
(3 Servings)

1 lb. chicken livers
3 green onions, diced
1 large green pepper, seeded and diced
6 large mushrooms, washed and quartered

1 large carrot, scraped and diced
1/2 small cauliflower head, broken
   into little pieces
2 - 4 tbsp. butter or margarine
1/4 tsp. ground ginger
1/4 tsp. thyme
1/4 tsp. marjoram
1 tsp. salt or to taste
1/4 tsp black pepper
1/2 cup sour cream
1 tsp. soy sauce
1 4-oz. can shoestring potatoes

Wash, clean, and chop your vegetables. Melt half the butter or margarine in a deep skillet and sauté the onion, pepper, and mushrooms for 5 to 7 minutes, sprinkled with the herbs, salt, and pepper. Now add the cauliflower and carrots and continue sautéing for another 3 to 4 minutes. The cauliflower should still be crisp to the bite. Push the vegetables aside, add a little more butter or margarine if necessary, and brown your chicken livers well—this takes about 5 minutes. Stir in the sour cream, flavor with soy sauce, and heat everything through, making sure you don't let it boil. Serve with the shoestring potatoes on the side and have some beer ready in the refrigerator. It goes very well with this.

Since you've been kept pretty busy fixing this, why not just have cheesecake for dessert—pineapple or cherry round out the colorful meal well.

CHICKEN LIVERS L'ORANGE
(4 Servings)

1 lb. chicken livers
4 tbsp. butter or margarine
1 inner heart of celery, diced
1 med. large onion, sliced
1/4 cup flour
1 - 2 tsp. curry powder
1 15-oz. can chicken broth
1 20-oz. can apple slices, drained
1/3 cup seedless raisins
2 tsp. dried orange peel
1 pkg. saffron rice
1 - 2 tsp. salt

Cook saffron rice according to package instructions. In a large skillet melt half the butter or margarine and brown the chicken livers in this for about 5 minutes, while you dice the celery and slice the onion. With a slotted spoon lift chicken livers out and keep warm on a plate, wrapped with aluminum foil, while in the remaining butter you sauté the onion and celery for about 5 to 7 minutes. Push vegetables aside, and stir flour and curry powder into drippings; when you have a smooth paste slowly add the chicken broth, stirring until smooth and thickened. Return the chicken livers to skillet together with the drained apple slices and raisins plus the orange peel—the kind you get in a jar on your grocer's shelf. Stir and let heat through before you serve with saffron rice and a glass of beer.

Since this dish is a little on the sweet side, follow it with a cheese tray, which also gives you a chance to use up the outer stalks of celery you didn't chop up. Cleaned and chilled they are great with cheese.

NOTES

A word of warning . . . I had to go into my den and repeat ten times the words of T. S. Eliot: "Humility is the most difficult of all virtues to achieve; nothing dies harder than the desire to think well of oneself"; before I could cope with the compliments heaped upon me after serving the next three dishes. Hope you fare as well.

DELICATE LAMB KIDNEYS
(2-3 Servings)

6 lamb kidneys
1 - 2 tbsp. flour
1/2 tsp. salt
1/4 tsp. black pepper
1 small onion, diced
2 tbsp. butter or margarine
1 8-oz. can mushroom pieces
1/4 tsp. sweet basil
1/4 tsp. nutmeg
1/2 cup juice from
   mushrooms
2/3 cup dry sherry
1/2 of 1 8-oz. pkg. egg noodles
Butter and parsley

Cook noodles according to package instructions. Wash and clean the kidneys, cut them in halves, and dust with flour, salt, and pepper, while in a skillet you're sautéing the diced onion in butter, under cover, for about 5 minutes. With a slotted spoon lift the onions out and keep warm, add more butter or margarine to skillet if necessary, and quickly brown kidneys over medium high heat, on both sides. Lower heat and return onions to skillet, together with the mushroom pieces and 1/2 cup of their juice, sprinkle with basil and nutmeg, give it all a stir, and simmer, under cover, for about 3 minutes, before you add the sherry; continue simmering under cover for another 5 minutes, by which time your noodles should be cooked. Drain noodles into a colander, return to their pot, and toss with butter and parsley before serving with the kidneys.

A crisp, green salad looks and tastes nice with this, as does a glass of beer. For dessert have some pastries from your favorite bakery.

LAMB KIDNEYS EXTRAORDINAIRE
(3-4 Servings)

    1 lb. lamb kidneys
    1 med. onion, diced
    3 tbsp. butter or margarine
    1/4 lb. cooked ham, in thin strips
    1 8-oz. can mushroom pieces, drained
    2 tbsp. flour
    1/2 tsp. crumbled bay leaves
    1/4 tsp. thyme
    2 tbsp. parsley
    1/2 cup orange juice
    1/2 cup port wine
    Salt and pepper to taste
    1 pkg. instant mashed potatoes

In a deep skillet melt the butter while you dice the onion; sauté onion in this for about 5 minutes, under cover, before you add the ham you've cut in thin strips and the drained mushrooms. Continue simmering under cover for 5 more minutes and now wash and clean the kidneys, cutting them in halves. With a slotted spoon remove the vegetables and ham from the skillet and keep warm, add more butter or margarine to skillet if necessary, and quickly brown the kidney halves you've dusted with flour. When brown on both sides, return vegetables and ham to skillet, sprinkle with thyme, bay leaves, and parsley, pour the orange juice and port wine over all, give it a good stir, and simmer, under cover, for 10 more minutes, during which time you fix the instant mashed potatoes as per package instructions.

Since this is not the heartiest of dishes and since you do have the time, you may want to serve the Danish Cherry Pie from Page 167 for dessert.

LAMB KIDNEYS STROGANOFF
(4 Servings)

1 lb. lamb kidneys
2 med. onions, sliced
4 tbsp. butter or margarine
2 tbsp. flour
1/2 tsp. thyme
1/2 tsp. marjoram
1/2 tsp. salt or *to taste*
1/4 tsp. black pepper
8 large mushrooms
1/2 tsp. prepared mustard (Dijon)
1 cup commercial sour cream
1 8-oz. pkg. egg noodles

While the sliced onion is sautéing, under cover, in half the melted butter or margarine, wash and quarter the mushrooms. After 5 minutes add mushrooms to the onion mixture, sprinkle with thyme, marjoram, salt, and pepper, give a stir, and continue simmering under cover for another 5 minutes, while you wash, clean, and cut in halves the kidneys. Dust them with flour before browning in skillet, and start your noodles cooking as per package instructions. When kidneys are brown, reduce heat, give everything a good stir, and let simmer, under cover for about 10 minutes before you add the sour cream and prepared mustard. Let it just heat through and serve with the drained noodles.

Cucumber salad goes nicely with this and if you want to serve it, start your dinner out by slicing the cucumber and sprinkling it with salt, before you put it in the refrigerator. When you are ready to serve, squeeze any extra liquid from cucumbers and toss with 1/4 cup vinegar you have mixed with 1/2 tsp. salt, 1 tsp. sugar, and 1/4 tsp. pepper . . . and bar from your house anybody who quotes that old ditty by R.H. Barham:

> *'Tis not her coldness, father*
> *That chills my laboring breast;*
> *It's that confounded cucumber*
> *I've ate and can't digest.*

The Thirty Minute Dinner

If we are what we eat, and if John Milton was right when he wrote: "The childhood shows the man, as morning shows the day," I should today be one enormous container full of calf's liver . . . one of my favorite foods since early childhood when I would even order it for birthday dinners — much to the chagrin of my guests, I might add. Anyway, on the next couple of pages you'll find some recipes for this delicacy, made a little more sophisticated than in earlier years.

CALF LIVER BAKE
(4 Servings)

1 lb. calf's liver, sliced
3 med. onions, chopped
8 large mushrooms, washed and quartered
1 - 2 tbsp. butter or margarine
1/2 tsp. marjoram
1/4 cup flour
2 1-lb. cans potatoes, drained
1 tsp. salt
1/2 tsp. black pepper
2 tbsp. imitation bacon bits
1/2 cup boiling water
1 beef bouillon cube
1/4 cup dry sherry

Set oven at 350° and take out 2 skillets. Chop the onion and wash and quarter the mushrooms while you melt 1 tbsp. butter or margarine in one skillet. Sauté onions and mushrooms in this for 5 to 7 minutes, under cover, with the marjoram sprinkled over. In the other skillet quickly brown in the remaining butter or margarine the sliced liver you've coated with flour, adding more butter as necessary. While liver is browning, grease a 2-qt. baking dish and drain the canned potatoes, cutting the larger ones in halves. In bottom of baking dish spread the onion-and-mushroom mixture, top this with the liver slices, arrange potatoes on top, sprinkle with bacon bits, salt, and pepper, before you pour over the hot water in which you've dissolved the bouillon cube and the sherry. Cover and bake for 15 to 20 minutes, during which you have time to fix a nice green salad, sparkling with cherry tomatoes.

Coffee and cookies are all you need for dessert.

CALF'S LIVER CALIFORNIA STYLE
(4 Servings)

1 lb. calf's liver, sliced thin
1 tbsp. flour
1/4 tsp. dry mustard
1/2 tsp. salt
1/4 tsp. black pepper
3 tbsp. butter of margarine
1 - 2 med. onions, sliced thin
1/3 cup hot water
1 beef bouillon cube
1/4 cup dry red wine
1 tsp. thyme
1 orange, unpeeled and sliced thin
Sugar
2 1-lb. cans potatoes, drained
Parsley

Mix together the flour, salt, pepper, and mustard on a small plate or piece of waxed paper. Melt 3 tbsp. of the butter or margarine and quickly brown the liver you've coated with the flour mixture. When nicely brown transfer liver to an ovenproof platter and keep warm in a 300° oven, covering the dish with foil. Add more butter or margarine to skillet and let the thinly sliced onion sauté in this for 5 minutes, before you add the wine and hot water, in which you've dissolved the bouillon cube. Sprinkle with thyme, give it a stir, and let simmer for about 3 minutes before pouring over liver in dish. Add more butter or margarine to the skillet, and brown well on both sides the thinly sliced orange that you have washed before slicing. Sprinkle orange slices with a little sugar before placing on top of liver, and keep warm while you sauté the drained potatoes in the remaining butter or margarine, tossing with parsley before serving them with the liver.

For dessert have a piece of your favorite cheesecake.

There is an old proverb, "A guilty conscience needs no accuser"; and I believe it was Gladstone who said, "The disease of an evil conscience is beyond the practice of all the physicians of all the countries in the world." Not that I have taken my particular problem to too many doctors, but it does seem that every time I have been penny-pinching on the main course, I become enveloped in guilt that isn't relieved until I've spent a little more on a dessert than maybe I should have. I've tried to figure it out, but have given up, deciding Oscar Wilde was right when he said: "The only way to get rid of temptation is to yield to it." So after offering you a really economical main dinner dish, I give you one of my favorite desserts and leave it up to your will-power to decide if you want to include it in your menu . . . but since you already have the oven going, why not?

LIVERWURST LOAF
(2-3 Servings)

1/2 lb. liverwurst
1/4 lb. ground beef
1/4 cup pickle relish
1/2 cup grated Cheddar cheese
1/2 cup fine dry bread crumbs
1 egg, beaten
Butter or margarine
1/4 cup water

Set oven at 350°. In a mixing bowl break up the liverwurst and mix well with the ground beef, pickle relish, cheese, bread crumbs, and egg. Shape into a small loaf and place in a greased baking dish. Dot with a little butter or margarine, pour the water into the bottom of the dish, and bake for 25 minutes. Serve with this:

QUICK POTATO SALAD
(2-3 Servings)

1 1-lb. can potatoes, drained
1 green pepper, seeded and diced
4 green onions, diced
1 - 2 stalks celery, diced
1/4 cup mayonnaise
1/4 tsp. dry mustard
1/4 tsp. dill weed
1 tbsp. wine vinegar

Put the drained potatoes in a salad bowl, cutting the larger ones into bite-size pieces, and mix with the other diced vegetables, before you toss them in mayonnaise you've blended with mustard, dill, and vinegar. Chill until ready to serve.

DANISH APPLE PIE
(4-6 Servings)

1 8-in. prepared graham cracker pie crust
1 8-oz. container cottage cheese
Nutmeg
1 1-lb., 4-oz. jar apple and pineapple sauce
Red currant jelly
1/2 cup butter or margarine
1 cup fine, dry bread crumbs
1 tsp. cinnamon

1 cup heavy cream, whipped
2 tbsp. sugar
1/2 tsp. vanilla extract

If the oven isn't already going, set it at 400°. In a small skillet melt the butter or margarine and brown in this the bread crumbs you have sprinkled with cinnamon. In the meantime, spread the cottage cheese in bottom of pie crust, top with apple sauce, dot with large globs of red currant jelly, and spread browned crumb mixture on top of this. Bake for 15 minutes and serve warm, topped with the cream you've whipped with sugar and vanilla extract.

Believe me, you won't mind you've got some left over —it's great any time of the day and night.

LATE SUPPERS

Over the door to Victor Hugo's study, the following legend was inscribed:

To rise at six, to dine at ten,
To sup at six, to sleep at ten,
Makes a man live for ten times ten.

Being an early riser myself I can agree with the first four words, but after that Mr. Hugo loses me. Trying as hard as I can, breakfast usually becomes a cup of coffee, lunch something I grab between appointments and—spending half my time working in live television and motion-picture production—dinner has come and gone in the form of too much coffee and odds and ends from a vending machine.

Agreeing wholeheartedly with Stevenson's statement, "A mortified appetite is never a wise companion," I

244 The Thirty Minute Dinner

have created some quick, nourishing, yet not too hearty dishes that I fix on such occasions, and I hope they'll come in handy for you on the days when you either stayed downtown for some late shopping, caught a 6 o' clock movie, or simply had to stay at the office way past dinner time. I guarantee you they won't give you bad dreams, and although you or your family may be sleepy and as divided as to what to do as the characters in the old nursery rhyme:

> *Come, let's go to bed,*
> *Says Sleepyhead;*
> *Tarry awhile, says Slow;*
> *Put on the pot,*
> *Says Greedy-gut,*
> *We'll sup before we go.*

everybody, you included, will feel better if you serve one of these easy, late supper dishes.

The first one is a good old-fashioned American corn chowder that does need your attention more or less for the full thirty minutes.

CORN CHOWDER
(4 Servings)

1 large onion, sliced
2 green peppers, seeded and
   cut in strips
2 - 3 tbsp. butter or margarine
2 large potatoes, pared and diced

1/2 cup water
1 tsp. thyme
2 tbsp. imitation bacon bits
1 chicken bouillon cube
1 17-oz. can creamed corn
2 cups milk
1 tsp. salt
1/2 tsp. pepper

In a large pot melt the butter or margarine while you slice the onion. Sauté this, together with the green pepper, cut in strips, for about 5 minutes under cover. Pare and dice the potatoes and add those along with the water, thyme, bacon bits, and bouillon cube. Give it all a good stir and let it simmer for about 10 to 15 minutes after you've brought it to a boil. Now add the corn, milk, salt, and pepper, and let heat through, but not boil ... about 10 minutes. Have some hard-crust rolls and sliced cheese on hand for those who like to have that along with their chowder.

This next recipe is a heartier version of the popular Denver omelet. It's fixed in a matter of minutes, practically, and delightful either accompanied by coffee . . . or glasses of foaming beer, because as Emerson so rightly said: "God made yeast, as well as dough, and loves fermentation just as dearly as he loves vegetation."

HEARTY HAM AND EGGS
(4 Servings)

1 large green pepper seeded and cut in strips
1 - 2 med. onions, diced
3 - 4 tbsp. butter or margarine
1/2 tsp. thyme
1/4 tsp. dry mustard
1 12-oz. can whole kernel corn
1 lb. precooked ham, cubed
6 whole eggs
1 3-oz. pkg. cream cheese
Chives
Hard-crust dinner rolls

Set you oven at 400°, or the degree required according to package instructions for the prebaked rolls, and heat them. Clean and slice the pepper, dice the onion, and sauté in the butter or margarine you've melted in a skillet, mingled with the thyme and dry mustard. In about 5 minutes the onions should be limp and translucent and it should be time to stick the rolls in the oven. To the skillet add the cubed ham and drained corn; let it heat through while you beat the 6 eggs with the cream cheese. Add egg mixture to skillet and scramble until eggs have your preferred consistency. Sprinkle with chives and serve right out of the skillet, passing the hot rolls around with it.

NOTES

The Thirty Minute Dinner

This next recipe for onion soup is somewhat heartier than what you may be used to. Incidentally, if slicing onions makes your eyes water, try letting the cold water run while you do it . . . it sometimes helps . . . or run the knife you're using through a slice of bread . . . that can do the trick too, not to forget the important discovery recently made at one of our universities that if you keep your mouth shut, your eyes won't water. I was not aware we all stood around gaping when we sliced onions . . . but who am I to challenge science? And just remember: "They that sow in tears shall reap in joy."

CREAMY ONION SOUP
(3-4 Servings)

3 med. onions, sliced thin
2 tbsp. butter or margarine
1/2 tsp. thyme
1/2 tsp. salt or *to taste*
1/4 tsp. black pepper
3/4 cup water
3/4 cup dry white wine
2 beef bouillon cubes
1 1/2 cups half-and-half *or* milk
Cheese croutons

In a large saucepan melt the butter while you slice the onions very thin. Let them simmer in this, under cover, for about 5 minutes, before you add all the other ingredients except the half-and-half. Give it a good stir, bring to a boil, reduce heat, and let simmer, under cover, for about 15 minutes. Now add the half-and-half or milk and continue simmering until just before boiling point, about 7 minutes. Serve piping hot with cheese croutons sprinkled on top.

NOTES

The Thirty Minute Dinner

This next favorite recipe of mine is not only great for a late supper... it does double duty substituting for canapes at cocktail time.

QUICK QUICHE
(3-4 Servings)

1 8-in. unbaked pie crust
4 slices of bacon
1/2 of 1-lb. can potatoes, drained
6 green onions, diced
3 eggs
1/2 cup grated Cheddar cheese
1 cup milk
1 tsp. salt
1/4 tsp. pepper
1/2 tsp. dill weed
Nutmeg

Set oven at 400°. While the bacon is frying to a crisp in a small skillet, chop the green onions and dice the potatoes. Spread onions and potatoes in bottom of pie crust, the kind you get at the store, crumble bacon on top of this, and sprinkle with salt, pepper, and dill weed. Break eggs into a small bowl, beat with the cheese, stir in the milk, and pour into pie shell. Sprinkle nutmeg on top and bake for 20 to 25 minutes, until egg mixture is set.

A frosty glass of beer is very good with this.

This last recipe is a variation of the popular English Yorkshire pudding, named, I believe, after the county Sydney Smith once described thusly to a friend: "My living in Yorkshire was so far out of the way, that it was actually twelve miles from a lemon." Obviously, lemons are not among the ingredients for this tasty dish that only requires your presence in the kitchen for about five minutes.

SAUSAGE PUDDING
(3-4 Servings)

1 lb. small pork sausages
3 eggs
1 cup milk
1 cup fine flour
1 tsp. salt
1/4 tsp. white pepper
1 tsp. ground cardamom

Set your oven at 450°. Brown the sausages in bottom of a flat baking dish, while in the blender you whir together all the other ingredients. When sausages are brown, pour off excess fat, cover with batter from blender, and bake for 25 minutes. Don't dilly-dally around at serving time or the dish will lose its gorgeous puffiness, but do have some beer on hand to serve with it.

The Thirty Minute Dinner

The ancient philosopher Plato once wrote, "The beginning is the most important part of the work," which is oh, so painfully true; but sometimes drawing it to its end can be equally difficult, as you begin to wonder if you said what you wanted to and included the things that were important and of interest—and there will always be different opinions as to that.

To those who'd prefer to see woman liberated from the "demeaning" work of house and kitchen, I can only quote Shakespeare: "He is well paid that is satisfied"; and William James: "A thing is important if anyone thinks it important."

And to those who see taking care of family and friends represented by Richard Crashaw's little poem:

Life, that dares send
A challenge to his end,
And when it comes say 'Welcome Friend'

I will quote Emerson's words: "To fill the hour—that is happiness." And according to John Masefield, "The days that make us happy make us wise."

If you only derive half the pleasure from using this book that I got from writing it, we should both come out all right—because in the words of George Bernard Shaw, "We have no more right to consume happiness without producing it than to consume wealth without producing it."

INDEX

BEEF
chipped, 69
ground
  beef Lindstrom, 112
  beefy spinach skillet, 71
  cheesy beef and noodles, 73
  Ernest Hemingway's picadillo, 77
  Frikadeller, 86
  hamburger pies, 84
  hamburger-vegetable
    casserole, 74
  Hungarian meatballs, 97
  Kima, 110
  liverwurst loaf, 237
  meatball stew, 95
  Mediterranean meatballs, 99
  Mexican meatballs, 101
  pantry stew, 80
  peanutty mini-meat loaves, 92
  pesky beef and macaroni, 82
  ricey meatballs, 103
  sauerbraten meatballs, 105
  south-of-the-border
    meatballs, 108
  special mini-meat loaves, 93
leftover
  hurry-up curry, 89
steak
  Alice's meaty sunshine
    salad, 114
  beef and cauliflower skillet, 64
  beef in sour cream, 60
  beef in wine, 62
  beery beef Stroganoff, 59
  deviled, 57
  Roquefort, 55
  round steak stew, 67
  skillet flank steak, 66
stew
  meatball, 95
  pantry, 80
  round steak, 67

BEVERAGES
buttermilk cooler, 116
rummy coffee, 78

CHICKEN
baked, 121, 131
Chinese, 124
with Chinese mushrooms, 126
creamy and lemony, 128
curried with broccoli, 133
dainty, 130
Mongolian, 135
ricey amandine, 138
ricey orange, 139
salad, 141

CLAM(S)
risotto, 16
creamy spaghetti, 46

CRAB
Piscean spaghetti, 48

DESSERTS
almond-applesauce bake, 75
apple-prune bake, 37
baked mincemeat peaches, 122
banana cream whip, 56
brandied strawberry whip, 145
chocolate pineapply rings, 192
Danish apple pie, 238
Danish cherry pie, 167
Danish jello, 88
dreamy strawberries, 136
flaming bananas, 100
flaming strawberries, 94
Liz' date pudding, 159
nut bars, 90
prune mound, 157
rummy coffee, 78
skillet apples, 80
strawberry-banana delight, 19

EGGS
curried ham and egg bake, 184
hearty ham and eggs, 246

FRANKFURTERS
chile, 150
chowder, 152
cornbake, 154
Pacifica, 158
risotto, 156
sauerkraut stew, 161

HAM
cubed
　curried ham and egg bake, 184
　curried ham pilaf, 182
　Far Eastern ham and rice, 186
　ham, cheese, and potato
　　bake, 188
　ham-vegetable bake, 189
　hammy baked beans, 191
　hammy green peppers, 193
　hearty ham and eggs, 246
ground
　Mediterranean patties, 220

KIDNEYS
lamb
　delicate, 230
　extraordinaire, 231
　Stroganoff, 232

LAMB
chops
　cheesy, 166
　Island, 169
　skillet stew, 170
ground
　Greek patties, 219
　pilaf, 172
　South African lamb bake, 176
leftover
　Indian lamb skillet, 174
stew
　skillet, 170

LIVER
calf
　baked, 234
　California style, 235
chicken
　jardinière, 226
　l'orange, 228

PORK
ground
  frikadeller, 86
  Mexican meatballs, 101
  porky meat loaf, 201
sausage
  porky spaghetti, 203
  sausage pudding, 251
tenderloin
  Hawaiian, 198
  Samoan, 196
  sweet and sour, 199

QUICHE, quick, 250

SALADS
Alice's meaty sunshine, 114
chicken-vegetable, 141
cucumbers with yogurt, 220
Greek tuna, 49
quick potato, 238

SCALLOPS
coquilles St. Jacques, 39
he-man, 18
supreme, 20

SHRIMP
avocado seafood shells, 42
curried à la U.S., 22
en papillote, 24
Stroganoff, 26

SIDE DISHES
cheese bread, 183
cucumbers with yogurt, 220
quick potato salad, 238

SOLE
bell pepper, 28
coquilles St. Jacques, 39
fillet à deux, 30
fillet delicieux, 32
fillet sauterne, 34
sole-ful broccoli bake, 36
speedy fish stew, 44

SOUPS
consommé au port, 25
corn chowder, 244
cream of celery, 173
creamy onion, 248
Danish consommé, 33
frankfurter chowder, 152
Greek chicken, 170
herbed chicken, 106
pea, 142
presto borsht, 43
tomato consommé, 40
wine consommé, 187

SPAGHETTI
creamy clam, 46
Piscean, 48
  porky, 203

SQUAB, sherried, 144

STEWS
frankfurter sauerkraut, 161
lamb chop skillet, 170
meatball, 95
pantry, 80
round steak, 67
speedy fish, 44

TUNA
Greek salad, 49
Piscean spaghetti, 48

VEAL
cutlets
  Austrian schnitzel, 208
  cheesy cutlets, 214
  Danish schnitzel, 210
  paprika schnitzel, 212
  piccata, 216
ground
  Greek patties, 219
  Mediterranean patties, 220
scallops, 217